READ THIS BOOK

This book is primarily recommended for able-bodied persons whose life circumstances prompt them to seek sources of inspiration, motivation, and creative change. It is also written to inform and inspire individuals, families, friends, and professional persons who serve people with disabilities.

This book is the true account of chronic quadriplegic Michael Schwass. Mike's uncanny motivation and relentless perseverance enabled him to achieve what was once considered impossible. His unyielding spirit attracted to him a bevy of athletes, motivational professionals, and philanthropists.

Through this labor of love readers will better understand and more effectively deal with the circumstances their life has handed them.

What others are saying about this book:

"This book should be read by everyone! It should be read by your kids, friends and parents that play sports. It benefits anyone who plays sports, plays the piano or is just able to walk and move."
— *Darren Pang, ESPN broadcast analyst*

"Don't Blame the Game" is a wonderful key for moving forward in life using the power of positive choice, particularly in the face of adversity."
— *Bill Campbell, Chicago, WLS-ABC-TV*

"What an extraordinary story! Michael set his sights on a nearly unobtainable goal and with his own special support team accomplished his mission."

— *James D.A. van Hoften, Former NASA Astronaut and Navy fighter pilot*

"Don't Blame the Game" affirms the human spirit and affirms us all."

— *Deborah Wood Holton, Ph.D., Associate Professor, DePaul University*

"The first time I saw Michael Schwass was when he was a sixteen year old young man, strapped to a hospital bed that turned him every 2-3 hours. I thought, "This person doesn't have a chance to go on with his life." Thankfully, this extraordinary man has proven me wrong."

— *Stan Mikita, NHL Hockey Hall of Fame*

"Don't Blame the Game" is graphic, straightforward, and heartfelt. It is a story about the power of a positive attitude, and how an athlete's competitiveness and drive can serve him when life deals a difficult blow."

— *Jack O'Callahan, 1980 Olympic Hockey Gold Medalist*

"Mike's book is an inspirational account of how the human spirit can triumph over the greatest tragedy."

— *Grant Mulvey, Former Chicago Blackhawks 1st Round Draft Pick*

"Reading your book brought back vivid memories of the long journey you have made to get back on your feet. This is a very inspiring story!"

— *Cliff Koroll, President, Chicago Blackhawk Alumni Club*

"Don't Blame the Game" shows what can be done if we take control of our lives and don't live a life of 'Blame'."

— *August Martinucci, M.D.*

"Mike's injury is a testament to the strength and magnitude of human endurance. His desire in seeking new treatment to improve his life and the lives of others, is truly inspirational."

— Dr. Samarjit S. Jaglan, M.D., Orthopedic Surgeon

"In an age when so many, with so much, are struggling, the time is right for people to hear Michael's story."

— Ross A. Hauser, M.D., Author Prolo Your Pain Away!

"Read this book! We can all learn valuable lessons from Mike's experiences."

— Dr. Ken Krebs, D.N., D.C.

"Mike's story is a roadmap of how to use self-discipline, determination and a laser-like focus to accomplish the seemingly impossible."

— Anthony R.. Galante, D.C.

"Mike's story helps me to understand the Gospel more profoundly. If I suffer with the Lord, God will raise me to new life. God has raised Mike to new life, and God's gift of Hope is renewed in me."

— Father Frank Keenan, Chaplain, Lutheran General Hospital

"Mike's story of triumph and continued efforts bring his inspiration to others!"

— Ron Holt, M.D., FACEP

"You will find strength, courage and passions as you read about Mike's journey, and you will never look at your own struggles quite the same again. . . a must read!"

— W. John Cox, D.C.

"Mike was a daily inspiration to Keith. He would be very proud of Mike for sharing his amazing story of strength and courage."

— Cindy, Kevin and Molly Magnuson

DON'T BLAME THE GAME

THE COMPELLING ACCOUNT OF
A QUADRIPLEGIC WHO TOOK
ON THE WORLD AND WON

And How You Can, Too!

Michael Schwass, MSW
Clarence Phillip Trausch, Ed.D.

© 2005

CONTENTS

DON'T BLAME THE GAME

THE COMPELLING ACCOUNT OF
A QUADRIPLEGIC WHO TOOK
ON THE WORLD AND WON

And How You Can, Too!

Michael Schwass, MSW
Clarence Phillip Trausch, Ed.D.

CREDITS
Editor: Nancy Butler Ross • www.TheBookMuse.com
Design: Anderson Designs
Typesetting: Cline Printing, Ltd.
Printing: Whitehall Printing Company

PUBLISHED BY
MSA Publications
P.O. Box 2973
Des Plaines, Illinois 60017-2973, USA

ORDERS AT
http://www.dontblamethegame.com

Copyright © 2005 by Michael Schwass • Printed in the United States of America
Library of Congress Number: In Publication Data
ISBN 0-615-12606-5

1. Self-help   2. Inspirational

ACKNOWLEDGMENTS

To name all the people who played a significant part in this book becoming a reality might be a book in itself. However, I especially want to thank Chris Cline of Cline Printing, Dave Alexander, Jeff Hirsch of Whitehall Printing Company, and David Anderson of Anderson Design. Appreciation to the folks at Ocean Hyperbaric Center/ Holiday Inn Lauderdale-By-The-Sea, Florida for their helpful nature, as well as Midwest Hyperbarics in Bolingbrook, IL. A special thanks goes to the Chicago Blackhawks hockey organization and the Chicago Bears football team.

DISCLAIMER

This book is designed to provide inspirational and educational information in regard to the subject matter that is covered.

It is sold with the understanding that the publisher is not engaged in rendering professional services. If expert advice is required, the services of a competent professional should be obtained.

Every effort has been made to make this book as complete and accurate as possible. However, this text should be used only as a general guide, and not as an ultimate source of information.

DEDICATION

This book is dedicated to two extremely powerful people in my life:

To my mother, the center of my universe, who showed me more courage and zeal for life than I will ever know.

To Keith Arlen Magnuson, and his immediate family, who exemplify love, motivation, and high ethical standards.

PUBLISHER'S NOTE

In December 1975, then sixteen year-old Michael Schwass sustained a devastating blow to his neck in a hockey accident, which left him paralyzed from the neck down for life: an instant quadriplegic. *Don't Blame The Game* is the chronicle of this indomitable youth who decided he would walk again, and the astonishing transformation that characterized his journey. Now in his mid-forties and living in Des Plaines, Illinois, Michael teaches and lectures to audiences all over the country, inspiring his able-bodied listeners with courage and skills to face and overcome their own challenges.

At the end of each chapter, Michael is interviewed by Dr. Clarence Trausch, his long-time life coach and coauthor of *Don't Blame The Game*. In these dialogues, Michael inspires the reader with wisdom garnered from a lifetime of harrowing experiences and remarkable achievements. His penetrating answers and charming manner hold a treasure trove of insights into the playoff of one of life's most horrifying trials, faced head-on by a stellar personality. What follows is an adventure story – and an opportunity and a formula for conquering your trials too.

AUTHOR'S NOTE
TO READER

by Michael Schwass

It is now the autumn of 2004, and twenty-nine years since I became paralyzed. The time is right for me to recount, for myself and for others, what my life has been over the past decades. I am excited about what I have to share with you. Students, friends, and even family have asked for it. Certainly, it has been an awakening.

After going through this writing experience with my long-time mentor and friend, Dr. Clarence Trausch, and then reading back through it, I get a new perspective on what I have accomplished. It is clear that all of my early decisions after my hockey accident and instant paralysis were based upon becoming more functional, getting up from my bed of pain, and eventually walking. Then, finally, attempting to walk independently, which is to say, without any support whatever. I would not change those decisions, or have let life's circumstances dictate what would become of me. Being involved and proactive, and taking action in the face of the forces of nature operating against me is my way. My intention has always been to pursue a better way of life.

On this journey, I did achieve most of my goals, in one form or another. I gained functional use of my arms. Then limited use of my hands. I gained the ability to brush my teeth, to groom myself, and dozens of other skills done in creative ways. Then eventually, I stood, and I walked. Mine has been a life filled with startling successes even in the face of deep tragedy.

Yet today, due essentially to the ravages of double-time aging and the onslaught of infections, I have come full circle, returning to my wheelchair. That is why my story has a bittersweet tone to it. The bitter part springs from my youthful realization that my circumstances could never be turned back. Once traumatic events are set in motion — a crushed spinal cord, for example — the body's fragility, its lurking mortality, becomes apparent. Having a condition or disease that places that mortality before one's face every day is very difficult indeed. Then after a time, a sense of absurdity of the body tends to arise and hard questions emerge. Why am I crafted in such a way as to come apart? Why go on living? Such thoughts can generate a kind of cynicism.

But, there is sweetness too. I can still experience the highs, even though I am increasingly restricted. I can and do enjoy sporting events, hockey games, rituals, weddings, movies, and other good times with family and friends. I have attained an advanced university degree, become a national speaker, and loved wonderful people. The danger to that human sweetness, for me, is straying from the present moment. Mentally drifting into the past, and away from my high-minded values and pursuits, opens the door to my lurking mortality and its relentless pursuit of me. These are the kinds of ongoing challenges that threaten my existence, and life's sweet moments.

Also, the process I have shared in this book reminds me anew that I live in the light. The way I have approached my challenges, and the transformation I have achieved, is more than just physical. It touches spirit, which in turn sheds a blessed sense of well-being and accomplishment upon me.

Although wounded and perhaps now somewhat overly cautious, I am a kind and sincere soul. I do not blame myself for the wounds, nor the caution, for they have served me, kept me alive in circumstances in which I had reason to be uncertain. Yet, caution requires energy, and has seemed to steal it from my kind and sincere nature. It is a trade-off, but one I must live with. As a quadriplegic, staying alive and out of trouble is a full-time occupation.

The best part, on this journey, is inspiring others, along with my own self, to be better just by doing their best with what they have been handed. The time is right.

AUTHOR'S NOTE TO READER

by Clarence Phillip Trausch

When Michael Schwass first came to me in February 1978 in Wheeling, Illinois, I was practicing psychotherapy, mind/body medicine, and applied philosophy; and teaching the principles of personal empowerment. I had also by then spent eight years as a religious monk, ten years as a criminal investigator, and long years of study with both Eastern and Western masters of meditation. In addition, I was deeply involved in motivational and inspirational education, presentations and seminars.

Michael arrived at my home office hunched low over his own lap in what looked to be characteristic quadriplegic fashion. His sister Carol pushed the wheelchair in which he rode. His short-cut sandy hair was neatly combed, and he wore a letter jacket that spoke of past athletic accomplishments. His young eyes, already heavy with years of sorrow, looked up at me with practiced wariness and penetrating intelligence.

I learned that he had become paralyzed over three years earlier as the result of a high school hockey accident. In spite of having spent those years in Herculean efforts to move, he had achieved little success, even after having pursued doctors and therapies across the country.

I also learned that he was medically diagnosed as a chronic quadriplegic — unable to any longer improve his functioning. In the accident at age sixteen, a blow to his cervical spine had crushed his spinal cord, creating a deep wound cavity in the vertebral structure. This damage blocked messages between brain and body below the injury at cervical vertebrae C4-5. His mind and brain could no longer signal his body to move.

Since the accident he had been in constant search of relief from his paralysis and pain, exhausting every medical avenue, but to no avail. Michael told me that he was not willing to accept the summary dismissal by doctors of his goal to walk, and that he had been seeking far and wide to find a coach, a mentor, maybe a miracle-worker, who could guide him to where he so greatly aspired to go.

His soft, emotionless voice belied the words of contempt he spoke for physicians, whom he held responsible in some practical and metaphysical way for the fact that he was still confined to this wheelchair.

"Every doctor I have seen has told me there is no hope of recovery below my injury. They are bastards, and they continually write me off and my hopes," he said.

I told him, "There are things you can do with that negative energy you are generating, and transform it into attaining your goal."

As we talked together during that first session, I increasingly realized that the soul that sat before me with penetrating eyes was a diamond in the rough, a precocious intellect with a steel will. Having dedicated my life to applying ancient wisdom to the problems of life, it was clear to me that Michael was demonstrating the emotional, intellectual, and volitional capacity to take on the gargantuan task he had set for himself. I became increasingly intrigued with this boy's potential, in spite of the impossible medical disability he presented. As I watched and intently listened, I decided on the spot that I would be one of those who would help him achieve that goal.

On that day we struck a deal and a bond and Michael began working with me, fortifying and preparing himself in mind and heart for the labor ahead. Any teacher or guide would be pleased to find such a worthy individual — one who responds to challenges, grasps difficult concepts, exerts every shred of energy, and then returns looking for more. How appreciative, then, is a teacher who finds such an attitude in one whose life has been utterly destroyed, and who yet comes back with the full force of intelligent and rock-hard perseverance. Michael Schwass was one such astonishing person.

The course of our work was and still is rewarding and fascinating twenty-nine years later. Each encounter with Michael is a metaphysical adventure, a launching of mind and spirit into the uncharted waters of possibility. Yet equally important is Michael's character — the psychology, the purpose, the spiritual connection, and the mutual appreciation and love. I have worked with a young man whose enormous strides set a high standard for wisdom, faith, and personal accomplishment.

Finally, the day came for him when his increasingly mighty will commanded his lifeless legs to move. And they did just that—lifted him from his wheelchair and walked for him. How that came to be, how we worked together, and how his soul transformed is the story you are about to read.

To my inner consciousness and spiritual work with him, Michael added the bodily component with his physical therapy teacher, Barbara Devine. Once the mind, body, and spiritual components began to integrate, it was just a matter of time before he stood and walked. Not surprisingly, Michael ultimately made the spiritual element the centerpiece of his life, acting from that perspective throughout the rest of his journey.

Therefore, in the process of writing this book, we have gathered a collection of wisdom principles that summarize how to live life successfully and how to become peaceful and satisfied in your life. Those principles have been placed in ordered form at the end of this book, called "The Four P's Formula." Scattered throughout the pages of this book in myriad ways, the principles are a recipe for effective living, and acquiring peace. It is because of the practical wisdom they contain that we have spent so much time developing, teaching, and presenting them to welcoming audiences.

Finally, over the years, I have encountered only a handful of individuals who have faced the challenges of their existence in the remarkable way that Michael has. He has not only been a student, but also a friend and teacher in return. The fact is, based upon his profound experiences and hard-won insights, he has become a sage guide for many, and this is in addition to the stellar character he has cultivated along the way. It is because of these many warmly inspiring reasons that he and I have agreed to write his autobiography together.

"Every blade in the field, every leaf in the forest, lays down its life in its season as beautifully as when it was taken up."
—Henry David Thoreau

INTRODUCTION: THE MEANING OF MY LIFE

I am coming to the end of my story and, perhaps soon, of my life. One of the major themes that occupy my thoughts in recent months is, I never thought my life would be this long. *How much more can I take? Do I want to go on?*

Increasingly, there is sourness to my existence because I more and more have to deal with the aging process superimposed on a crippled body. Although I had attained my goal of walking, it has not been without great cost to me and to many others in my life. I have a hip that is disintegrating, with barely half a femur remaining. This is due to ongoing degeneration that is a consequence of both a virulent staph infection, and the double-speed at which a quadriplegic ages. That accelerated aging by itself places me almost in my eighties, even though I am in my mid-forties.

I think also about my advancing arthritis, which is part of the cost of immobility; the disfiguration, and the unrelenting pain I am in. Pain is there, throbbing and unyielding in every joint, every hour. Keeping the pain manageable is what motivates me to exercise. The irony is that people think I work out so hard because I am some kind of a special and highly motivated person, when it is really all to "save my ass." In the beginning, it was just to impress doctors and to keep the momentum going toward my goal of walking. Now it is survival. I must admit that keeping myself alive is a mighty motivator!

The quality of my life becomes quickly stunted if I don't exercise and keep abreast of supplements, vitamins, medications, exercise, and all the bio-rituals I must go through in order to navigate a day. Regardless of the mundane character of these ceremonies, somewhere deep within my core I still have not lost the flame of hope that one day I will walk again, and perhaps walk independently. This is where I play a fantasy game with myself: that a cure for chronic spinal cord injuries may come to pass. The ultimate reversal! Perhaps a new femur head, or a fixed joint replacement. It is this oft-visited visualization that keeps me going. It is huge.

About every five years I hear that in five more years there will be a cure. I must keep telling myself that they just might come up with a gene, or a growth factor that will restore my crushed vertebra. This is my current corporeal purpose, the primary one that carries me onward each day. In my mind I say, *Every research center offers hope and hope does not disappoint.* There is a lot to be said for that phrase. There it is. The game I play. Hope.

Otherwise, if I were not acting on that hope, which accounts for a great portion of my ability to continue on, physical, mental, and social conditions would be much worse in my life. I am afraid that without the level of hope I must generate, my deplorable conditions would squeeze me into a different mind set, one in which I would be pursuing any viable way to exit my body and this earthly realm.

My ready justification for even entertaining leaving my body goes like this: *A body generally lasts 70, 80, maybe 90 years. Even though people can live such long lives, by the time they are in their 60s or 70s, some cannot even get around any more. For me, the fight has gone on for almost thirty years from my youth, and I have been breaking down miserably for the whole time. In the Spinal Cord Society literature it says that spinal cord-injured people age two years for every one year of a normal person. According to this formula, I am now 76 years old!*

If I did not have hope at my beck and call, my mind would be focused on how to escape having to endure any more of these trials. In my worst moments I consider just lying in bed and not eating or drinking. I imagine letting my joints freeze and my organs quit, and telling everyone to leave me alone.

On the one hand, those thoughts bring me an option, and in an ironic way, a feeling of relief and consolation, for they return some power to me. On the other hand, I think that this would be giving up, and letting a lot of people down.

Although these existential reflections bring me renewed motivation, doesn't there come a time when each person must entertain end-of-life thoughts? How much suffering can a person take? And, why should they have to take it?

I think of Jesus. He lived thirty years in relative quiet with an apparently good body. During his last three years, he traveled and taught, but without any physical horrors. Then, at the end of those three years, he suffered dreadfully for the last few days, and his life was quickly over. Jesus knew when he jumped on the borrowed ass and rode into Jerusalem that he was going to endure this torture. He knew that the whole cult of the physical body was futile. My guess is that he knew very well that he would do better for himself and others on the other side of this life. And, that his life on earth would be a legacy. Certainly, as he rode that donkey into Jerusalem, he knew he was going to die. But he did it anyway. He had had enough of his life and chose the time to go, by himself.

I also get consolation from the idea, that at some point I will have the same insight as Jesus. And, that if I am not taken by some infection or organ failure, I will come to realize when it is my time to depart and end my suffering. The gift of the insight that he had was to know when his time was up, and I believe that I, too, will receive that gift. He had to know this strongly in order to so intentionally welcome the ignominious experiences he had in his short life.

In addition, if Jesus was in fact human as well as divine, he must have had awful fears and confusion about his impending crucifixion, as would any man or woman. I have my own concerns over death, but much more so about the process of dying, which is more frightening than death itself. A prolonged illness and continued suffering are things that are more worrisome to me than actual death. Staying alive in such a weakened and perhaps helpless state, wherein I cannot control my functions or circumstances, is what disturbs me when I think about it.

Having done my first graduate internship in a nursing home, I witnessed people lingering on for up to ten years as human vegetables. This disturbs me! My placement job at the nursing home was to counsel and console the staff. As part of that assignment, I also got to deal firsthand with nursing home patients who had lost their rational thinking capacity, or whose bodies were rotting away even as their full conscious awareness lingered on. During this initial intern experience as a budding social worker, I stared futility in the face. My mind searched: *What is this living about when we are all going to decay? What is the meaning of this sad end?*

What I am about to tell you now is the answer to that question.

PROLOGUE

I came awake in blackness from what seemed to be a bizarre dream. An overpowering apprehension gradually arose in me as the drowsiness cleared. Nothing stirred. I seemed to be facing into deep, black space. As minutes passed, my eyes began adjusting, and peopled the darkness with shadows. I had no sense of where I was, or how long I had been there. A deafening stillness loomed in my ears. My usually acute senses seemed unable to decipher the scanty information they were receiving, and the trepidation in my chest swelled like a river in flood.

Then, in the twilight, I became aware of a glow to my left. Automatically, I began to turn my head in that direction to see what this soft light was. Nothing happened. No movement. My face remained where it was, fixed on the blackness. Mounting anxiety gripped my chest along with a sickening dread. Generated by my brief but disturbing experiences of the past few moments, a creeping awareness arose and spoke in my head—*I cannot move my body!* Instantly, the implication behind those words morphed into an even more distressing idea—I have no body!

My eyes rolled in a motionless head, searching in panic for some point of reference that would discredit my fears. It was then, out of the corner of my left eye, that I was able to catch just a glimpse of the source of the glow to my left. It was what seemed to be the moon, and the stars twinkling their lights in a sea of blue-black night. Confusion spread through me like a creeping chill, but did not remain in its form any longer than the earlier sensations. Before I could begin to conjure what was happening, I heard a soft voice call out, "Star?"

The sound of that voice touched somewhere deep within the now fragmented core of my being, and an angelic sweetness and peace welled up inside me. Now I thought that perhaps I was not alive at all, but maybe dead. Once again, I intended to move, to see what it was that had made that enchanting sound, but nothing happened. *Panic!*

Again, the voice called out, "Star?"

Now, the panic itself shifted into a kind of bewilderment. I considered: *Maybe I am alive!* In this mixture of urgency and confusion, I called back to the voice, uncertain of where the sounds came from, "What time is it?"

The voice answered, "It is the witching hour."

This response had an intense effect on me and turned my thinking back on itself again, *Oh, God! I'm dead, and I am drifting somewhere in the universe. I'm among witches, stars, moons, flashing lights, and darkness—and I can't feel my body!*

With no time for me to process this, I saw a person who did have a body emerge from the darkness and begin to speak to me: "You have lived through your operation, but you will be paralyzed."

Nowhere within me was it possible to grasp the implications of those words. Nothing registered in my brain at all. Yet, slowly and spontaneously, rising from a deep and hidden pool, sorrowful tears rushed forth, flooding my eyes. I began to weep.

"Life is either daring adventure—or nothing."

—Helen Keller

1

IDYLLIC DAYS

It was a cold December day in 1975. In the chill and darkening late afternoon, white snow lay about the neighborhood yards in huge drifts. Along the side streets, including my own, the snow had been dyed dirty gray by the passing cars, and in places tan patches of dormant grass testified to an earlier, warmer life. The trees spread their branches against a subdued sky, and the firmament was a slate, marbled in various shades of gray and punctuated with black and blue blemishes. Out of that ominous sky, snow was beginning to fall in huge white flakes, and my excitement ran high. I was sixteen years old, and come that evening I would play my twentieth hockey game of the season.

It was always the same. I would go down to the basement and pack my hockey bag. All my gear was there, including a set of weights and a trapeze. It was almost like a professional's locker room, even having a shower. After every game, I would hang all my gear up to dry. Then I would also clean my skates and re-tape my sticks. Dad made sure I did that. I had a little locker in a corner of the basement and a closet where all my hockey gear was stored. I took one of the sticks out and studied it. *This is the stick I will use tonight.*

My athletic equipment meant a lot to me. I had summer jobs in Des Plaines, Illinois where I lived. I worked both as a maintenance boy at Rand Park, and as a gas station attendant at Higgins & Harlem Shell Station. Making only about $2.10 per hour, I still saved everything I could squeeze out of my checks. When I had accumulated enough money, I bought myself the ultimate equipment, a new pair of hockey skates called Super Tacks. I loved those skates and felt like superman when I wore them, since most of my other equipment was used.

Hockey was not just another game to me — it was almost my whole life. I was good at it, and by my senior year in high school I had become one of the highest scorers in the conference and quite possibly the whole state. I was never able to attend hockey camp in Minnesota or Canada like so many other, maybe better, hockey players. Nevertheless, I did save enough beyond the Super Tacks to buy myself a spot in a new hockey camp that had opened in the nearby town of Niles.

Besides getting myself into the hockey camp, I used to sweep the floor at the local ice rink. The sports complex manager would give me some free ice time to get out my Super Tacks and practice improving my weak areas — stops, turns, and corners. I was fanatical, wanting to be the very best, so I made use of every minute the rink manager gave me. What I was doing must have worked, because for most of my high school and public league career, I was the hockey team captain or co-captain. The daily public address announcements at school often included some mention of what I had done in the latest inter-school competition. Kids would sometimes tease me, but I liked it, and I felt like a star. In those years my self-image grew by the hour!

Since several hours remained before the game that evening, my girlfriend Jill and I decided to go shopping at Golf Mill Mall in Niles. We spent most of the time looking for a birthday gift for my best friend, Dave. When I got home, Mom reminded me that I had a head cold, and urged me to skip that evening's game. No way! I was having an outstanding year and wanted to stay on a roll. Additionally, the team we were playing against was Glenbrook North High School, our archrivals in the Chicago Metropolitan North High School Hockey League. My school, Notre Dame Catholic High, was in the Triple A Red Division, which is the highest designation possible for a high school in the state of Illinois. We *wanted* that title. I *had* to play.

Although hockey was always my first love, it was the competition itself that was both my strength and my weakness. Basketball, football and baseball came easily to me, and I was recognized as skilled in each. Always putting forth my best effort in those sports, I appreciated my friends and schoolmates letting me know they recognized my ability by flashing warm smiles and shouting friendly greetings. But it was hockey that owned my heart. I suppose that was because I was so much better at it than the other sports, and I was considered a luminary. I knew it. And I basked in the light.

Growing up as I did along the banks of the Des Plaines River, there was plenty of Midwestern ice available to use for free. My Dad and neighborhood friends had taught me to play hockey when I was a little boy. Dad had preceded me at the game, playing semi-pro hockey for the Chicago Planerts, a local company that made hockey skates. After school each day, and on weekends, Dad and I played on the frozen Des Plaines River. We were often joined by an assortment of "River Rats" who, like me, could not afford to play on the expensive indoor rinks. So the river became our icy playground and as I grew, my natural athletic ability soared.

On those idyllic days, we loaded up a wooden crate, bulky with shovels, hockey equipment, jackets, thermoses of hot chocolate, and extra gloves. Then we gleefully pushed this contrivance bearing our precious cargo down the frozen river, looking to get a game going with other neighborhood hockey-heads. Spotting some boys, one of us would challenge them to a game. In our neck of the woods, we were something special on the river ice and seldom lost any games. A whole decade earlier my older brother Jim had played this same pastoral scene out on weekends with his friends.

For Mom, I seemed to be the focal point of her life. Being the youngest, and with one other sister at home, I got a lot of attention. So, with all my activities, the spotlight was often on me. The funny thing is though, I was never told I was good at what I was doing. Never told I was appreciated. Rather, I received routine reminders from both parents that I was not good enough; that I had not done enough, and had not lived up to certain expectations. These frequent infusions of inadequacy deeply affected the course of my young life, generating within me an abiding need to be the best.

On one occasion as a young boy, I was the starting third baseman and an all-star player with the Des Plaines Little League. Before the game, in full uniforms, we all stood at attention at our positions in the field listening to the National Anthem. The stands were full of parents and friends, and I was so proud of myself. We later won the game, reason for even more celebration. My Mom appeared on the field within a few moments, and said, "You are the only person on the team with hair sticking out of your hat. You are going for a haircut right now."

In spite of these lovingly misplaced priorities, I did know that I was valued. But the words were never spoken, the affirming gestures never given.

My Dad was a steady man, a quiet, hard-working tool-and-die maker. He was also shrewdly insightful about life and what it really took to survive. He labored long hours and spent little money. He lived life with a bare-bones mentality, and virtually never attended parties or entertaining events — except my hockey games. He tended to be aloof and to hold onto his thoughts and words until he gauged that the moment was right to speak.

Mom, on the other hand, was outgoing, a pretty and gregarious attention-getting woman who longed for a career of her own. A stable, fundamental Catholic woman, she eventually became an administrative assistant in the Archdiocese of Chicago. From her start there, she was always involved in the Council for Catholic Women, and was president of that organization for several years. It was an original Catholic feminist group, and a force to be reckoned with.

My siblings included five wonderful and loving sisters, and a brother fourteen years older than me who was my hero from childhood onward. Except for my sister Joan, they had all long ago launched their lives and had careers of their own. Jim, my only brother, was a super achiever and always on the move. He rode the crest of life and seemed to me to live on the cutting edge. Having a natural capacity to live life successfully, he shared his secrets with me. He always seemed to know a little about everything.

For example, Jim often worked three jobs to make ends meet. He was at once a security guard, a trucker, and a schoolteacher. He modeled for me that you did whatever it took to get something done. Like Dad, he would look for the best prices in stores, cut out coupons, and save his money. If need be, I learned, you swallowed your pride and worked at whatever paid the bills. For a time, he was a security guard for the Deep Tunnel Project, a flood failsafe development in Chicago, which diverted overflow sewer water into a storage facility, even though he had a degree in education. I thought he was much better suited as a teacher!

My girlfriend, Jill, was a pretty, brown-haired girl, petite with a well-defined figure and a dynamite personality. She had a manner of expressing herself that produced an enchanting smile that I loved. Although a year behind me in school, she trumped me in personality. Where I was reserved, she was outgoing and always happy. Jill came to every hockey game and was an avid supporter of mine. I

had dated before Jill, but no one seriously. She was my first significant woman, after Mom, and we had been together for about two
years. She attended Maine East Public High School, which was just
a few miles from the all-boys Notre Dame High School that I
attended. Jill was a treat, joy bubbling out of her all the time. And
she was always on my side no matter what happened. Her charming
personality endeared her to everyone, especially my team members,
who loved to joke and laugh with her.

During my years at Notre Dame Catholic High School in Niles,
I played hockey and during the first quarter of my senior season had
managed to become one of the highest scorers in the state. Also, in
my senior year, I began to get letters of inquiry from colleges invit-
ing me to play hockey on their teams. Remember, I was a still an
early aged senior at just sixteen! By late October my ability had
improved to such a point that coaches from other schools would
caution their players to beware of me, to "stay on Schwass" during
games, and to keep me off balance. I enjoyed the celebrity status
and the strength I felt in my body. Jill liked it too. Life was good.

To continue the story, skip the Interview and go to the next Chapter.

INTERVIEW

Dr. Trausch: Michael, you've had quite an incredible life as a quadriplegic. How would you characterize your life before that accident?

Michael: I had a good life. I was a healthy adolescent boy with a good family. On top of that, I had an unusually athletic body. Because I could feel that capacity and energy, I naturally began to take more risks, even though most of my activities were centered on bodybuilding and hockey. This life was good enough that I was not interested in becoming an attorney, doctor, accountant, musician, tradesman, or anything of that sort. I just wanted to play hockey, and I believed that playing would at least get me through college. I had no other goals in life at that time, and hockey consumed my thinking. I felt like Fonzie on Happy Days.

Dr. T.: You say that although hockey was always your first love, it was the competition that was both your strength and your weakness. Tell me what is hidden in that statement.

M. S.: What I was alluding to was that it kept me away from some normal social development, movies, library, theatre, and other important experiences. I was hooked on it like a drug.

Dr. T.: Do you believe that it was an addiction?

M. S.: Yes. I did not want to let go of it because it gave me so much power and esteem, and the future opportunity to profit from it, as well. So, I abandoned social life in general. Not with Jill, however. She was a hockey fan, so she fit in and liked the primary and secondary benefits. At dances or proms she was with a prominent guy. My parents also basked in some of my limelight. Their foremost group of friends consisted of hockey fans as well. So, everyone about me approved of and supported my addiction.

Dr. T.: Is this different than any other addiction?

M. S.: It was a good addiction for me. Through it, my identity grew. Because of it I was saved from other, perhaps destructive, paths like being a gang member, or a pitiful groupie of some star. Athletes are looked upon with great admiration. If a kid is going to get addicted, let it be to sports. At the very least it builds character, teaches us how to win and lose, how to deal with life and prepare for the troubles that are sure to come.

"I don't claim to have controlled events, but confess plainly that events have controlled me."

—Abraham Lincoln

2

TAKING FLIGHT

The Chicago Metro League hockey game between Notre Dame and Glenbrook North High Schools was set to begin at eight that night at the Northbrook Sports Complex ice rink. It was the twenty-second game of an eighty-game season, and as we drove to the Complex, the adrenaline pump was surging inside my body.

Earlier in the school year, during the first game of the season, a player from an opposing team crosschecking me had slammed me in the face with a stick. I took great umbrage and liberty with that insult and got into a boxing match with the offender. For my trouble I was promptly tossed out of that game and the next one as well by the referees. Although tonight was our twenty-second game, I had only played in twenty, due to that fight.

What would hockey be without a boxing match? But it does not take much reflection to realize that crosschecking, thrusting a hockey stick held in both hands out and across an opponent's face, is a recipe for disaster. This illustrates the more aggressive style of hockey I played. Anytime I saw a chance to check an opponent on the boards, I took it. This move entails skating into an opponent who has control of the puck near the rink's boundary walls, and aggressively shouldering him away from the puck.

It had been the same in football for me. I enjoyed these forceful and competitive moves. Like the young rams and bucks in the wild, I was blowing off my excessive adolescent testosterone.

Jill and I rode in my old red 1963 Dodge Dart, with a push-button transmission and a rebellious starter. Mom and Dad drove separately. We arrived at approximately seven-thirty. I gave Jill a hug and headed for the locker room to get suited up while she went into the bleachers to search out my parents.

Hockey is a rough sport. That's one of the reasons I like it so much. Players needed plenty of safeguards against taking a puck in the face, or being checked — that is, rammed into the sideboards. We had been taught to prepare ourselves for the checking that is part and parcel of hockey, and to layer in protection. We were instructed, for example, to get our gloves up in front of our faces if we were going to make entry into the boards. That is an insider way of saying someone has checked you.

Just two weeks prior to this game, we had played in a Thanksgiving Day tournament with four other teams, including one from Green Bay, Wisconsin. One of their players had crosschecked me in the face and bloodied my nose. This time, not having a chance to start a war, I was taken to the emergency room and ended up needing several stitches on my face. Was it a problem for me? No way. *This is what the professionals do. This is what the Chicago Blackhawks do. This is kind of cool,* I thought. I considered myself "hot stuff." Dad told me my face looked like ground beef.

My team had two coaches. The head coach, Jim Meyer, was tall and lanky and had played and coached many kinds of sports in a variety of schools. His true love, however, was hockey and he desperately wanted to win a championship. He was a well-respected man in the hockey community, but he did not communicate very well with his players. And because he was a disciplinarian, many of us took what he said too seriously. He would sometimes become angry over things like players not wearing the right color socks. He would yell at us for not avoiding being checked. Some players enjoyed his anger, and used it to create a kind of comedy routine. Together as a team however, we respected his motives and did a good job for him on the ice. Honestly, I believe he loved us, because he would help us through trying academic and social times in school at Notre Dame. Sometimes, he would pull special favors for us.

Once I was having trouble in math. To be candid, I was actually terrible in algebra and geometry, and was close to failing. We had to "make grades" and maintain a passing average. Otherwise, ending up on academic probation, we could not play sports at all. Somehow I received a passing grade. More than once, Coach Meyer would knock on one of my instructor-priest's doors and ask for a private conversation with me about some team issue. This special treatment promoted an aura of my importance to the priest and the school. And, if the priest wanted to stay in good graces with coach Meyer, he knew he should do whatever he could to help me pass the course.

My other Notre Dame coach, Gary Weber, was a player's coach. He was easygoing, could talk a teen's language, and could translate the head coach's directions into terms that we could more easily understand. He was extremely well liked and had earned our admiration and trust. He was a cross between Eric Clapton and Scotty Bowman, the former head coach of the Montreal Canadians. He was like a Rock-and-Roll guy who had been pulled out of a band and enlisted into hockey. He could not skate very well, but he was allied with the boys. If we had any problems we were afraid to take to Coach Meyer, Coach Weber would do that job for us. Then we did not have to watch Coach Meyer go through his temper tantrums. What a neat system!

As was the custom at Notre Dame before every game, my team members gathered in a group, held hands, and said a prayer to the Blessed Virgin Mary asking for her protection. At the end of the quiet prayer, Coach Meyers said aloud, "Queen of Peace, pray for us. May no one be seriously injured in tonight's game."

The game began on time, and I was starting, playing center forward. I was wearing a white jersey with blue and crimson trim, topped off with green numbers. I had an extra "A" on the front of my jersey, indicating that I was an alternate team captain. Cool colors. Notre Dame was a classy school and I was proud to play for them.

As the competition commenced, the other team descended on me right away. Two Glenbrook players had been directed to shadow me. I felt them hovering about me as I glided over the ice. They were like mosquitoes, each one carrying a long wooden proboscis, waiting to land and sting if I didn't keep moving. In spite of those offensive players, their defensemen seemed to play it differently. As I approached, they let me enter into their own zone, backing, backing off. Perhaps they had thought I would cut left or right. Then, there it was. I saw an opening straight ahead of me, and I rode my Super Tacks right down the middle, lifted my stick back and waist high to my right, and slammed a shot straight into the net. The goalie never touched it. The crowd shot up and cheered. I was Superman. The defense had backed up for me, let me into their zone, and effectively given up the fort.

It is common for defensemen to challenge an offensive at their blue line, for that line represents the boundary to the last third of defensive ice, inside of which is the defense's goal. That territory needs to be protected at all costs. Because of how it went down, I felt a sense of respect from those players, as if they were overawed by my status, which had been accruing during the last dozen games. They were defeated by their own perceptions!

Before the first period ended I had scored two goals, each time Glenbrook's defense letting me draw in a bit too close to their goal. I was thinking, *Gee, this is getting too easy!* The other team's offensive members had been working on me, battering me, knocking me off balance, ramming me into the boards, determined to keep me from scoring. I expected this, and even enjoyed the idea that I was the focus of their concerns. How I loved this sport!

Just then, I received a loose puck that had come careening off the sideboards. Luckily enough, I picked up the puck with my stick, and maneuvered around two opposing players, including one last defenseman who challenged me at his blue line. As I got into position to take a shot at the goal, a star Glenbrook player plowed into me from behind, striking me hard on the upper torso and the back of my right shoulder. Taking flight, I rocketed toward the end boards. There was no time to react and get my gloves up in front of me. The momentum of my full one-hundred-and-fifty pounds served solely to hammer my face into the end boards. Like Raggedy Andy, I landed crumpled in a heap in the corner of the rink, life as I knew it had been unalterably shattered.

To continue the story, skip the Interview and go to the next Chapter.

INTERVIEW

Dr. T.: What was it about Notre Dame that was classy to you?

M. S.: It had high academic standards, a great sports tradition, and was held in very high esteem by other schools. Also, its being a private institution seemed to set it apart from other schools.

Dr. T.: Being educated at a Catholic High School, was the prayer, so plainly expressed at the game, a part of your private life?

M. S.: No. I didn't get very involved with religion at that time, even though I had been an altar boy. I didn't throw myself into Catholicism as many others did. Perhaps, I should have paid more attention to religion, which would have better contributed to my overall personal, mental, and spiritual development.

Dr. T.: How did your girlfriend, Jill, perceive you?

M. S.: She saw me as a star, a handsome guy who was "with it." She had a healthy sense of her own identity, her own self-esteem, and shared it with me, treating me as an equal.

Dr. T.: You seem to have brought an attitude to hockey with you. What was that aggressive style of play all about?

M. S.: That was my own nature, and therefore my approach to sports. In the game of hockey, if you were not aggressive, you would soon be gobbled up and spit out by an aggressive player!

Dr. T.: Did your parents encourage your athletic prowess and your style of play?

M. S.: A lot of it was self-motivated. Some of it was out of the anger of not being anybody, wanting to be good at something and being recognized for it. I don't recall any parental influence on me, other than their problems. But, neither one of them was aggressive by nature.

Dr. T.: What was it about the hit you took from behind the night of the accident that told you something different had happened?

M. S.: When my head and face hit the boards, I was just beginning to get my gloves up in front of my face to protect myself. It felt like someone had slammed a door into my face, but the blow was humongous. That hit so vibrated, and rattled my head and body that I knew something very bad had happened.

Only those who will risk going too far can possibly find out how far one can go. Humankind cannot bear very much reality."
—T. S. Eliot

3

A WILD RIDE

The moment I was hit, I knew this was a blow like I'd never had before. A driving pain pierced my neck as the bones of my vertebra shattered and blasted like shrapnel into my spinal cord. For a timeless few seconds I lay still, on my back, on the ice. Then a bizarre sensation came over me. Although no one was near me, I felt like someone was pulling my arms and legs up, toward the stadium's rafters. My nervous system was short-circuiting. Coach Weber came out onto the ice from the sidelines, looked down at me and said, "Can you get up?" I said, "OK, I'll get up, if you'll just pull my arms and legs down." Although I clearly recall saying these words, one of my teammates on the ice that night, star player and alternate captain Tony Salemi, told me later that I was trembling, and that my eyes had rolled back in my head so that only the whites were visible.

At that moment, I was on the vague border between reality and shock, and fast entering into the latter. What was going on in my mind was that God or the angels were pulling my arms and legs toward the sky, but my back was staying flat on the ice. I looked up toward the roof beams and saw a glowing radiance replacing those rafters coming down upon me. I now believe I was having a near-death experience. But it did not dawn on me at the time, because my obsessive connection to my body and to the physical world was so fierce.

If this was not bad enough, without forewarning, I felt a hot poker shoot down my back, and the glow from above became more intense. Some significant time must have passed, because I next became aware of being jarred by the paramedics who had arrived some time earlier. This jostling pulled me back to my body. I was cold. They must have known, for they covered me with blankets. Next, the paramedics carefully placed a wooden backboard under me. People were talking in hushed tones, but I was not really there. Rather, I was back with the light, in a place of suspended time. Slowly, I do not know how much time passed, the light faded, and I was again lying on my back with a crowd of people staring down at me. I thought again, *If someone would just pull my arms and legs down, I will get up.* However, my arms and legs were not up in the air! A sickening realization of what had happened to me, *I have been rammed into these boards,* reappeared like a specter from the shadows of my mind, and my thoughts began to race ahead. *There has to be something they can do when I get to the hospital, like give me a hot bath to make this pain go away.* I heard one paramedic say I had a sore neck, as he packed ice around my neck. Although I was now in full-blown shock, some clear inner eye remained silently watching, and I became aware of a hushed atmosphere about me. As I lay on that ice, a crumpled form all dressed up in my bright costume, rescue workers spent another ninety minutes working to stabilize me. Eventually, the emergency team was able to gingerly lift and usher me to a waiting ambulance, while in the stadium a pall remained over the crowd.

The sirens proclaimed our coming to everyone within a half-mile as we pulled out of the ice arena. Mom rode with me, and I recalled that in times past, when we were somewhere together and heard an ambulance siren, she would say, "Whenever you hear an ambulance, make the sign of the cross and pray for whoever is in there." Well, now it was my mom and me in there. Here I was, a sixteen-year-old boy with his mother, and we were now the ones riding that ambulance!

Suddenly, Jill came to mind, as we sped through the streets. Where was she? What was she thinking? She was so loyal to me, I was sure she would be upset. Then the people in the stadium came to mind. What must they be thinking about me? That I was badly injured, needing an ambulance to whisk me away so swiftly?

During that tumultuous ride, I found myself playing over and over in my head the same hopeful sentence that I had fashioned as security at the rink: *I am sure there is some kind of hot, electric bath they can give to make this pain go away, and get me moving again.*

As the ambulance shrieked our urgent passing to the city, I was pulled from my reverie by an itch on the tip of my nose. I said, "Mom, will you just scratch my nose." She reached over from her bench seat beside me and scratched it. I would not appreciate the significance of that simple request, and that small act of my mother, since it didn't mean anything to me at the time. It was my mom being Mom. I had it wired in my brain that when we got to the hospital, they would fix me, and I'd be okay.

I think back, as I say this, to when I was a little boy. Mom would take me to the doctor and treat me with special attention so I wouldn't resist or cause any trouble. After being examined, if I had been good, we would go out for a soda. Tonight it was like that again. I was going to the doctor, and here was Mom by my side, taking care of me. When we are done, I'll get a milkshake and get back to the game.

I had nothing by which to gauge this new experience, beyond measuring it against those early homey, boyhood medical experiences with my mom. She was the center of the solar system of my family and friends. She was the one who had taught me everything, except sports. How to cook. How to iron. How to sew. How to clean the house. I could not go out on Saturday until all my chores were done. She was a stern Irish woman, but I appreciated her knowledge because, in the bigger picture, she was teaching me how to live.

In the emergency room at Lutheran General Hospital in Park Ridge, I was transferred from the backboard to a wheeled gurney, and rolled into the emergency room. An emergency room surgeon checked me, using pins to prick my skin and determine whether or not I could feel anything. I could not. But, he was aloof and with-drawn and did not talk to me. Then, without a word to me, he sent me to the X-ray department. When the films returned, an on-call neurosurgeon came in and said to me, "We've got to operate on you immediately. There is internal bleeding, and you have a fifty-fifty chance of living through the night. Do you understand?"

I thought he was joking. This cannot be happening to me, not to my body. Urgent thoughts rose up to defend me, *I might die! How stupid is that? I got banged in a hockey game and I am going to die? This doctor is a madman.*

My distressed mother said to me, "Michael, let them do whatever they want."

Within no time at all, a priest appeared, apparently out of nowhere, wearing a stole and said, "I'm here to give you your Last Rites."

I almost laughed out loud. I was a Catholic-educated kid. I knew what the Last Rites were, and that they were only given to people who were near death. *How did this priest make such a horrible mistake?* I said, "Father, you and the doctor have the wrong room. There is someone hurt really bad in the next room." I could not in any way get hold of the idea that this was all about me. I was watching a movie. This was a dream. This was not real!

> "*This sixteen-year-old patient* [Michael Schwass] *had fractured his neck this evening in a hockey game, and became quadriplegic. Because of the grave, serious nature, a long discussion was held with both the mother and the father – in the presence of several sisters and his brother – relating to the risks and details of attachment of the tongs and also the need for cervical laminectomy in order to free up a severely compressed spinal cord.*
>
> "*No guarantee was made at any time, and the parents were told of the sometimes fatal, serious, long-term prognosis for this type of catastrophic injury. In a final effort to save this patient's life, consent was obtained for immediate surgery. However, due to the unstoppable continuous internal bleeding and the religious denomination of the paralyzed individual, the on-call pastoral chaplain was notified STAT. Before proceeding with the operation, the patient had received his Last Rites.*
>
> "*Preoperative Diagnosis: Complete quadriplegia, secondary to cervical fracture dislocation; C-4 & C-5, with subluxations and severe laceration of surrounding ligaments.*" --Neurosurgeon Dr. Louis Amador, M.D.,

Lutheran General Hospital Report of Operation, December 1975

Once the priest did his "ritual thing," the surgeon and my mother were back on me about having the operation immediately. I considered what they said and thought, *OK, I'll have this surgery, and then I will be back to the way I was. Let's get rid of the pain. Let's get this surgery over with, and then I can get back on the ice.*

As soon as I assented, without any hesitation the hospital attendants wheeled me into another room, where I would have one of the most horrifying experiences of my life. With no ability to move, out of the corner of my eye I watched a nurse lubricate a long rubber tube and then inch it into my nose. I must rephrase that. She barely lubricated that tube, and then drove it up my nose! I was such a quick and responsive athlete, and now I could not even turn my head in reaction to this insult. Having been spared prior bodily troubles, I was oblivious to any kind of limitation. I was immortal. This nurse could have plucked my eyes out and I could not have stopped her. Due to the nature of the emergency, most of the hospital people Mom and I had encountered seemed less than compassionate.

Next, in order that my neck and head remain absolutely motionless both before and after the operation, a team of doctors appeared who told me they would drill holes into my skull. Into these holes they would fit stabilizing bolts. A virus of apprehension grew in my mind as technicians moved about me with their tools. Then without any warning, they began. One-by-one they drilled two deep holes into either side of my cranium, and I cried out, begging them to stop. The shriek of the drill overpowered my cries and I screamed louder. The scent of burning flesh mixed with the reek of hospital odors wafted into my nose. Out of the corners of eyes pooled with tears, I could see the ceiling tracks of the drapes that separated the patient spaces. Why I looked at those tracks, I don't really know. Maybe they were a way I hypnotized myself with focusing. Overpowering my focus on those tracks, a voice playing in my head demanded attention. *How could anyone be doing this to another human being? How could anyone do this to another person who is awake?*

As I endured the torment, held down by nothing more than my own body's paralyzed carcass, it was as if my brain matter was being twisted on that drill bit, and roasted as the hot shank did its menacing work. The drilling lasted for what seemed an eternity. This one ruthless event traumatized me beyond what I could have imagined. When the cacophony stopped, a nurse pushed a syringe into an IV port connected to my left arm. I felt the roiling cauldron of terror that had been cooking in my chest begin to cool, and my ready-to-break tension dissolved into sweet oblivion.

To continue the story, skip the Interview and go to the next Chapter.

INTERVIEW

Dr. T.: That night of the accident, was there anything you could point to that contributed to this accident?

M. S.: My stardom was reaching greater and greater heights. My name appeared among the highest scorer lists. It was happening for me. People would cheer when I skated onto the ice. Local radio stations would broadcast my games play-by-play, and the commentators repeated the name "Schwass" often.

Was life too good to be true? Too good to be true, for me? Was there something in my nature or family character that would not allow for such success? Did my core self-worth not match what was in the offing for me? It seems so, now, as I think about it.

Dr. T.: You told me that you did not panic at any time during or after crashing the boards. Is that true, or were you hiding it?

M. S.: I had a high regard for the medical profession, and believed that they would be able to fix me. I never had even heard of such a thing as paralysis. Besides, the paramedics had told me while I lay on the ice, that it was just a sore neck and would eventually go away. I did not know enough to be in any panic.

Dr. T.: So, you were not aware of encountering your own death?

M. S.: Lying there, the rafters above me seemed to drift away. The intense arena lights baked my eyes. At the time, I did not recognize it because it was not in the public's awareness, but it is likely that I was having what is now defined as a near death experience. Based upon the significant amount of internal bleeding, and the multiple lacerations around the bony structures in my neck, it is quite clear that I would have died without the surgery that night. I had no awareness of it.

Dr. T.: Was this accident the first you had ever had?

M. S.: I had an injury my junior year, which cost me about eight weeks off the season due to an ankle injury. My heart was broken; I wanted to play so badly. It was tough emotionally to attend and watch the games from the sidelines.

Dr. T.: How is it that being home grown, so to speak, around religion and priests, that in the hospital you dismissed concerns of both the doctor and priest for your ability to stay alive?

M. S.: I was so caught in my own powerful self-identity, I could not believe even them, that I could be so mortally wounded. Also, the shock of such a rapid injury did not give me time to accommodate to this very new idea. Finally, perhaps I can attribute it to the strength of the human spirit in its quest to survive.

"Wonderful and terrible trial, from which the feeble come out infamous, from which the strong come out sublime. Crucible into which destiny casts a man whenever she desires a scoundrel or a demigod."

—Victor Hugo

4

INTO THE NIGHT

I awakened to a swarm of images vying for attention in my sluggish brain. Before they could congeal and make some sense, I heard a vaguely familiar voice say: *"You have survived the operation, but you will be paralyzed."* Hearing the words was equivalent to being told I was Mickey Mouse and lived on the moon. I had no standard against which to measure them. How ironic, then, that as those words were spoken, the lyrics from a song by the rock group "Tears For Fears" arose in my head, *"Welcome to your life, there is no turning back."*

The nurse who had delivered the devastating post-op message to me might as well have plunged a dagger into my solar plexus while smirking down upon me. Now, in thinking back on that lifeless demeanor and tone, I can see more of what might have been going on for the nurse. How does one deliver such a message, "You are alive. But you will never move again." Then however, I could not let the meaning penetrate my defenses. The notion that I would never again move my body under my own volition had to be absurd. The rule in my world was, bad things don't happen to good people. I was a star. I would be laid up a few days and then get back to my stardom. All the ingredients for horror were there. Fortunately, shock, otherwise perilous, was shielding me against what would have been a mounting psychosis.

The day that followed the accident was filled with residents and doctors visiting all day, testing me with needles, questions, each demonstrating perfunctory interest. How did I feel? How much pain did I have? I appreciated even this paltry attention. It kept my mind working on something vital. I was alive. It was all I had.

As the minutes turned into hours in this state on the border between muddy consciousness and feverish reverie, I came to learn that I was confined to what is called a Stryker frame. It was a con-trivance molded from the torture chambers of the Spanish Inquisition. The frame is composed of two long boards. The back piece is a long, body-length plank about three-quarters of an inch thick, and six feet long. The front piece has the same dimensions, but has a small, face-sized hole in it on one end so that the patient's forehead and chin must both rest against it, permitting an opening just big enough for the eyes, nose, and mouth to fit into it. The chin rest was a sliding contraption to accommodate differing face lengths. The boards had been brought together, with me in the middle, to make a human sandwich, and ropes were tied around the two sandwich parts to hold my "body-meat" fast. I lived in this apparatus, looking out through my stockade-like window for hours on end.

I was turned like a carcass on a spit every two to three hours, day and night. A team of nurses would loosen the head brace and turn me, only to reapply the tension as soon as I was flipped. I had to ask aides to please *gently* loosen the head mechanism, because that loosening action so close to my ears, sounded in my head like someone smashing metal garbage can lids together in an alley. It reverberated through me like an earthquake. Mostly, the nurses paid no attention to my requests, and would be even more aggressive in their manner.

Rigged to the head brace was forty pounds of cervical traction designed to stretch and separate my spine, so as to limit swelling. Each time the aides turned me, the forty pounds tugging at my head was released. The shock of this maneuver sent a wave of nausea through me, and I would throw up. I remained imprisoned within the confines of this giant rotisserie day after day, night after night, for weeks on end. The traction cords stretched from the top of my head outward gave the impression of a man being hanged, sideways. What is most prominent in my memory about this time is the flipping, flipping, flipping — now the floor, now the ceiling, now the floor.

My minute-by-minute entertainment while facing upwards was counting each acoustical hole in the ceiling tiles. When facing downwards I prayed, *Our Father, Hail Mary, Glory Be,* all while surveying the fluid that trickled from my nose and pooled onto the floor. Frequently this view was blurred by my tears, which dripped into a sticky mixture twenty-four inches below my face. Desolation was slowly consuming my heart. Sorrow was my companion. Time was torturous. My young body used to move in swift synchronicity with my mind, and it was a thrill for me. With the slightest hint of intention, I could hurl a ball, slam a base hit, receive a pass, and my body-vehicle would do it all seamlessly and effortlessly. Now, the wheels of my mind were in hyper speed, and my body was on dead stop. The dissonance that this caused in me was dreadful. *I wanted to die.*

Punctuating this madness were visits from my family and friends. But, because I was in intensive care, only family members were permitted to visit. Mom and Dad came, and Jill was there too, considered by hospital staff as a family member. Jill was wonderful, and her short visits sitting with me were the highlight of my day. She was crafty, however, and never mentioned what she must have known: that I was paralyzed for life.

Mom and Dad's visits were wonderful also, and it was good to see them. They would talk a bit more than Jill did about the game and the accident, without getting into too much detail. Although I had these visits, I could not see the people who visited me, since I was in the Stryker frame, and could not turn my head side-to-side. I could only look straight up, or straight down, depending upon the position of the frame.

One day, about a week after my accident, while I still endured this torment, Dave Alexander, my long-time and best friend, who had been trying to get in to see me, succeeded. Since I was in the intensive care unit with a "no visitor" designation, Dave was told he could not visit. He must have prevailed upon someone on staff, for they eventually let him in. As he tells it, when he saw me he was overwhelmed. My Stryker bed had just been turned 180 degrees so that I was facing down. Dave's shock was obvious to me, for he did not know what to say or do. After recovering to some extent, he quietly moved closer to me and gently lay down on the floor so that he could see my face. When I saw his open and compassionate expression I knew that he would listen to me.

"Hello, Dave."

"Hello, Mike. What's this like?"

I held back the tears. "It's terrible. I can't move. People tell me I'll never move again. They turn me every couple hours. I can't believe this is happening to me."

"Yeah, I can't imagine what it's like."

As pregnant moments passed in silence, and Dave looked up at me from the floor with wide eyes, I saw my chance. "Dave, will you slide the chin rest on this board I'm lying on up a few inches so that it will cover my face and stop my breathing? I don't want to live like this anymore." I was thinking, *I can't believe I am going through this.*

It is so far-fetched, so unreal. I want to be done with it. I want to die now, and Dave is the best chance I have of pulling it off.

Dave did not answer right away. Finally, he said quietly, "Everything's going to be okay. Don't worry."

When I heard those soft, confident words, they sent a glimmer of hope into my desolate heart. I grasped at them, a terrified child clutching its security blanket.

When Dave left, I was again alone. I did not do what one would call sleep, for my mind was constantly aware of the bizarre situation I was in. Shuttling between razor sharp wakefulness and torpor, I endured the night. At seven the next morning, a nurse entered my room to tell me that Mom called to check on me. In order to talk on the phone, an aide would hold the handset up to my ear. It was an awful experience, because the contact was never really good, making it difficult to hear. But, it was good to know that she, or that anyone for that matter, was thinking of me.

I knew that I was utterly dependent upon other people. There is no way to communicate the range of feelings I navigated over the early days to deal emotionally with this state of affairs. Eating, or rather, feeding time, was one example. During mealtime I was placed downward on the Stryker Bed, my face about two feet from the floor. A nurse with some Jell-O or other soft food would come to my Stryker rack, sit on the floor beside me, and spoon some food up into my mouth, which along with my eyes and nose, peeked out at her through the hole in the board. This was the only position in which I could eat since in any other one I would be at risk of choking.

Three weeks of this ordeal and a second major cervical operation had passed since my accident. Night turned into day, and back into night again. The Stryker frame flipping continued. My soul was still in shock, and ghastly thoughts ran through my head, as if trying to find some tolerable resting place. Would I remain fixed in this Edgar Allen Poe nightmare forever? Would I wither and waste away as days and nights merged into timeless waiting? Would I go insane from the tide of abandonment rising in my throat? Although Jill and my family were still visiting me, those short visits did not serve to satisfy my senses and mind.

One night while these images raced, I was distracted by a chunky *"thump"* to my right, and the image of a heavy slab of meat hitting the floor formed in my mind. An alarm shot through me, adding itself to my earlier feelings and images. Before I could begin to conjecture, a light went on in the room, and a voice called my name, "Michael?" With the help of the light, I realized I was staring at the floor, having lost track of my time and place location in space. The voice that had called my name said: "Michael, your arm dropped off the board. I'll put it back on for you."

For the first time since being told I was paralyzed for life, a bit of what had unfolded became a terrifying actuality. I had evaded the advancing assault of reality on my sensibilities with all manners of deflection, refutation, denial and contrivance. Now, my own arm, the one attached to my own body, had slammed onto the floor, and I was not even aware of it. I had not even felt it! Not only was I paralyzed and unable to move at all, I was numb. My body, as far as my mind knew, did not exist!

Until my arm fell, I had lived in the security that I had an athletic body and superior prowess. I had also carried the idea that medicine and doctors knew everything and could fix anything. I also maintained strong attachments to my life of hockey, dating, and school. These were tough resistances to acknowledging the reality of what had happened to me. But with this small sound of my arm falling, the sturdy defense I had in place trembled, and a wave of lethal doubt rolled through my core.

To continue the story, skip the Interview and go to the next Chapter.

INTERVIEW

Dr. T.: Was your arm dropping off the Stryker board and onto the floor without you knowing it a turning point for you in the reality of your situation?

M. S.: I think it was just the beginning of my awakening to my predicament. Being in the state of denial, I never realized that it was a serious injury because I had never known of such a thing as paralysis. I never had met a paralyzed person. I was an ignorant teen. A considerable undoing of my denial occurred when my arm came loose from the Stryker frame, and like a roast falling out of a refrigerator, slammed onto the floor. That event at first frightened me, and then made me very sad. One day, soon after the accident, another turning point in understanding my situation happened. My older sister Carol, who was a nurse, stated an obvious fact when she said, "You have sustained a serious injury, Mike." But her voicing it at that moment, even though I was fully aware of it, produced a measurable increase in my understanding of how my life was unutterably altered.

Dr. T.: You had an important youthful belief: "Bad things don't happen to good people." Is that still true for you today?

M. S.: I think it was a religious thing, gleaned from being an altar boy. If you do good things, good things will come back to you. All the ritual around that, getting up to serve six-thirty mass for so many years, how could anything happen to an altar boy? Today, I have lost faith in that principle. I still believe in God, but not that he or she will take care of me in such a way that nothing bad will happen to me. There must be some other, larger system operating, perhaps a cosmic dance or play going on, the purpose of which is not entirely clear to us. I don't know that anyone knows for sure what the plan is. Perhaps a few highly evolved beings do.

Dr. T.: You talked about having taken more risks as your adolescent body developed. Do you see any philosophical or metaphysical connections between your risk-taking and the accident?

M. S.: I did think I was indestructible, and until the accident I was always pushing the limits of physical capacity. This might have reflected some hidden self-destructive tendencies. I may have been getting back at my parents for not directly acknowledging my many accomplishments. In my mind they were getting their own needed recognition through me. I am sure it was all unconscious on our parts, but I must have picked it up at some level, as they showcased my accomplishments. I was the welcome distraction in their lives, and a means for them to avoid facing themselves and what needed attention in their marriage. Today, almost three decades later, having an extensive background in psychology, I can clearly see the connection. The excess that I contributed to the sport of hockey was generated by the latent resentment I had. They had used me to avoid facing their own relationship difficulties, and also to gain some vicarious pleasure from my athletic successes.

Dr. T.: What is more difficult to endure, revisiting with me the horrifying aftermath of the accident, or the unrelenting everyday problems you must now put up with?

M. S.: Certainly it is the everyday predicaments I encounter in navigating life. The horror and shock is in the past. I don't often revisit that experience except when people ask me about it. Then I am able to do it without a problem. But, to become entangled in that place of terror is a deathtrap. More difficult are the daily mental tensions: who will get me into bed; who will help me to the toilet; how will I endure another infection; what are the massive amounts of drugs I must take doing to me; will I have enough money to keep this life-production up? It is a full time job just to stay alive, let alone prosper.

Dr. T.: When you reflect on your experience in Lutheran General Hospital the night of the accident, is there anything that you would want to change?

M. S.: Looking back, I feel sad that they did not know as much about spinal cord injuries when I was injured, as they do now. I wonder, did the paramedics prepare me the same way they do a spinal cord injury today? What if they had flown me to a better medical facility, or provided me with a better surgeon? Today they tape your head down when they suspect a spinal injury. I could have incurred more paralysis-making damage in transport to the hospital than I sustained on the ice rink. The deficiencies in medical technology at the time sadden me the most. I don't dwell on that, because that is what could have been, not what is.

*"Kindness is the language, which the deaf can hear,
and the blind can see."*

—**Mark Twain**

5

DANCE OF THE CLOWNS

I had never understood words like kindness, compassion, and concern. Not really. How could I? I was a child. What possible education could an egocentric adolescent, recently delivered to planet earth in the form of a boy, get that would teach understanding of the plight of other life forms? And, even though I was in a Catholic high school that embraced the timeless values of goodness and compassion, I did not "get it." Maybe I had been absent the days these subjects were taught. Or, more likely, I was there, but failed to pay attention, so engrossed was I in getting what I wanted. It seems to me that only longsuffering, handicapped, damaged people are capable of seeing through the illusions of life that so mesmerize the healthy. Now I am one of those wounded people, and I see. My needs went from big items, to small ones. From fancy cars, colleges, and expensive hockey equipment, to how to get a straw into my mouth, and how to relieve painful cuts in my forehead from the

Stryker frame.

In the early days of my stay at Lutheran General Hospital, all the while being in the intensive care unit, a doctor came in with a pair of glasses and put them on me. They had an angled mirror system built in that enabled me to see a bit of a program on a television that someone brought into my room. Who would watch TV that way, catching a scrap of a program, behind and to my left, out of the corner of my eye? I would! That gesture was enormous for me. How could anyone who was not in my position appreciate the magnitude of that simple act?

I could, literally, not move a muscle, let alone my hands or fingers. I might have been mistaken as a corpse! When my nose dripped, I had to ask for someone to come and wipe me. Each time I was thirsty, I had to ask for water. Every time I was fed through the hole in the board, I had to express how to prepare my food. Something as simple as wanting salt. Pepper. "Would you please put some salt on the potatoes? Could you please put less food on the spoon?" Hundreds of things I had taken for granted, and had quickly done for myself, I now had to ask for. And, I had to ask kindly. I learned to behave in ways that would tend to get what I needed. I had to be patient. Gentle. Kind. Soft.

I also learned I would not get things just when I wanted them. When I asked, I could not hold an expectation that the outcome would be the way it would have been had I been able to do it for myself. People would do things in ways that were unexpected. If I asked for a bite of potato, I might get two foods mixed together, or way too much food for my mouth to accommodate. If I asked someone to move my arm, it might be moved beyond where I had envisioned, or in the wrong direction, leaving me uncomfortable. Although I could not feel on the outside, I could feel quite acutely on the inside. If I asked to have my nose scratched, it might be done so lightly as to create even more of an itch. These frustrations continued, unabated, almost moment-to-moment, and left me restless.

All too often my autonomic nervous system would go into crisis mode. Central nervous system paralysis causes that. It throws the autonomic system into shock. Since the autonomic nervous system regulates digestion, elimination, heart rate, respiration, sweat, temperature, and blood pressure, disturbances in it can produce life-or-death moments. One night I had my first encounter with this "bio-mischief." It began by my body becoming so cold I shivered uncontrollably. The room was warm, but there was no getting my body warm. And, nothing I tried to do with my mind, telling myself *I must be warm, the room is warm,* would stop it. The first time it happened, this frightened me terribly. Then, as I became all too familiar with such organic system shenanigans, I would get angry. *Why me in this absurd state of affairs? What a mad circus this body is! And, what doctor-clown is going to come in here next and perform some outlandish act? How long do I have do endure this?*

Experiences such as these were my steady companion at Lutheran General Hospital, and they weakened my adolescent conviction that I would get better. The turning and praying, counting and crying, watching and waiting, went on for the next few weeks. During that time, doctors were attempting to evaluate what had actually happened to my spinal cord, and just how bad the damage was, even though I had already been told that I was going to be a life-long invalid. I did not, could not, believe this prognosis. No amount of reasoning helped me to appreciate what had happened to me, or what my life from this time on would be like.

About two weeks after the ambulance had sailed into the Lutheran General Hospital emergency room with Mom and me, a buzz began among the staff. It climaxed with Dr. Goodlove, a pediatric physician, appearing at my Stryker bed. With a name like "Goodlove" how could I go wrong? Actually, it seemed to me that a number of doctors who worked with me had names that suggested that they would be able to cure me. Was this unfamiliar tendency to make meaningful connections a trick played by my frantic psyche? Was I so desperate to keep some thread of hope alive as I moved from one frustration to another that I created meaning?

Dr. Goodlove informed me that, after conferring with other staff surgeons, they had collectively decided that I had the best chance for recovery by being sent to John Wesley Hospital in Chicago. At John Wesley there was supposedly a doctor named Paul Meyer, an orthopedic surgeon who could fix my unstable spine.

From that small bit of information the gossip ran like water. Dr. Paul Meyer, God's gift to creation, would fix me. I blossomed with hope. This is all I needed. Let's get to John Wesley and get the job done!

Although I could hardly wait, I was afraid of Chicago. The big city was so different to me than the small suburb where I knew everyone. I also knew that people would not be able to come to see me if I was so far away. I was afraid of the unknown. Would I have to go through all the testing and probing I had endured at Lutheran General Hospital? I hoped not. How wrong I was.

To continue the story, skip the Interview and go to the next Chapter.

INTERVIEW

Dr. T.: What have you learned about kindness from those days when you were so newly paralyzed?

M. S.: Because of my desperate state, I learned to do whatever it took to get my needs met, and I discovered that kindness could be used as a mechanism to get that accomplished. Since kindness was expressed so infrequently by the hospital staff, I used it to motivate people to provide something that I needed. Kindness was better used in that way than not.

I experience the world as being full of care and compassion. I get letters from many places, drawings from children, after I speak about spinal cord injury prevention. These expressions are consoling. I see that eventually, understanding is achieved, and somehow a mystical network of love and kindness is functioning. This is the way I choose to see the world.

Dr. T.: Do you still get these autonomic nervous system disturbances where your system is thrown into disarray?

M. S.: Yes. Autonomic hyperflexia. Blood pressure rises, perspiration increases, and a pounding headache attacks my brain. These symptoms can be set in motion by a bladder obstruction, a bowel impaction, or from pressure on a body part that I cannot feel and therefore do not know is undergoing increasing stress.

Dr. T.: Do these episodes catapult you onto the brink of death, as in one having a heart attack?

M. S.: Certainly. A bad case of hyperflexia feels like someone has placed my neck in a vice and my head is going to explode from the increasing pressure. It is a recipe for stroke. When it happens, I immediately think "I am going to die." If it is not treated quickly the headache itself will knock me out. In my growing confusion and pain, I think the pounding cannot get any worse before I die. Hyperflexia is not the only event that can bring a quadriplegic to the brink of death. Pneumonia, the renal system shutting down, or a quad with a high spinal injury choking can do it as well. During my hip infection in 1997, for example, I had temperatures of 105 and 106 degrees. During such episodes I question how much more of this kind of assault on my body I can take.

"A pessimist sees the difficulty in every opportunity; an optimist sees the opportunity in every difficulty."

—Sir Winston Churchill

6

THE DUNGEON

Within five days of hearing of Dr. Meyer, on a Sunday morning in late December, I was loaded up, Stryker bed and all, into an ambulance and carried off to John Wesley Hospital in Chicago, where I would stay for two to three weeks for more surgery. Traveling with me were Mom and two other family members. It was a cold winter day, and the ambulance driver seemed destined to fall victim to hitting every pothole in the roads of Cook County. Each jarring shook the ambulance, sending a tremor through my neck and the wooden Stryker frame I was strapped to, demonstrating the unyielding quality for which it was made. Even though I could not see out of the windows, in my mind I imagined the cracked and dirty streets pocked with gaping holes anticipating our wheels. In spite of this assault, I could not complain. We had heard that Dr. Meyer was a crackerjack, the head of orthopedic surgery, and just the king of spinal cord injury cures. The staff at Lutheran General made him out for us to be godlike. He was going to be my savior. Dr. Paul Meyer would take this pain away. He would make me stand upright and walk out of his hospital. He would make my neck right again. Little did I know that this would be the first of my many expectations that would be ultimately dashed on the hard floor of medical reality.

After an eternity, we arrived at John Wesley Hospital, right at the lakefront on Chicago's Lake Shore Drive. It was a rude awakening for me. This hospital, unlike Lutheran General, was old, dirty, and gray, a fitting tribute to the typical Chicago skyline. It was connected both materially and therapeutically to the Rehabilitation Institute of Chicago (RIC), so that the two seemed essentially interchangeable.

Another shock to my sensibilities occurred immediately upon entering the hospital. This was my first encounter with African-American people. I don't believe I had ever talked to an African-American person, or knew about their culture, their oppression, and now I was to be living with them. Back at Lutheran General, in spite of the dreadfulness of the situation, people occasionally treated me like a star, a hockey athlete. Here, I was no longer a specialty. In fact, I was little more than a vegetable. All I could do was hear, think, talk, and blink my eyes. I was just another invalid. How would I ever guess that my torment was just beginning?

After being taken out of the ambulance and placed on a gurney, an orderly wheeled me into a filthy four-bed room (called a quad room). It reminded me of being in a MASH military field hospital. The cleanliness and antiseptic scene I had become used to at Lutheran General was replaced by dirty walls, sweat, body odor, old cleaning fluids, and musty spaghetti mops in a reeking concoction that caused me to retch. I lay in that room for a long time, waiting. Eventually, a nurse's aide came in and rolled me out to have more x-rays taken of my neck. At that time, the shadowy basement passageway was grimy, and filled with old elevators, mildew odors, and stained and decomposing concrete walls. The brew of trenchant odors in this cavern was overwhelming. The darkness, and the silent aides hovering alongside my bed, frightened me.

> 1/21/76 "This patient is a seventeen year old boy who was injured in a hockey accident on 12/3/75. He was immediately rendered quadriplegic and admitted to another hospital where a compression laminectomy of C4 through C7 was done an at that time a neurological examination revealed quadriplegia. Patient was subsequently transferred to spinal cord unit at Wesley Pavilion and then transferred to RIC [Rehabilitation Institute of Chicago] for further treatment."

Staff Chart Notes Taken the Rehabilitation Institute of Chicago

Within a few days, in early January, and after my status evaluation, the famed Dr. Paul Meyer prepared to perform surgery on my neck. Dr. Meyer was a tall, well-built man with salt and pepper hair, beginning to bald. His face was intense and stern, as he ordered staff members about. I thought he was brash and self-absorbed. However, the way he was talked up at Lutheran General Hospital, I figured he must have to be good at what he does.

In that operation, just over one month after my accident, I had my third major surgery on the bone and spinal rubble that lay at C 4-5 in my neck. Dr. Meyer worked to stabilize my posterior cervical spine using wire and bone graft. He removed a section of bone from the tibia in my lower leg, split it in two, and laid each half on either side of the vertebral body surrounding my crushed spinal cord. His intention, and hope, was that this would support what remained of my spinal cord, and bolster my neck. Although Dr. Meyer had his hopes that such jury-rigging would work to hold me upright, the clear impression he gave was that I would never walk again.

Before the operation, hospital staff had not even been able to place me in a wheelchair. After the operation, staffers moved me from my Stryker frame and into a soma brace, a padded, cage-like contraption around my head and neck to hold me upright. To an observer, it looked like a wire frame wrapped about my neck and head, with shoulder supports strapped tightly around my chest. Although this was a variation on the Stryker frame prison from which I had so recently been extricated, I was glad to be out of that contraption, and hopeful now of eventually being able to sit in a wheelchair.

The crucial and ongoing need for that support following the operation, posed problems of its own. I can even now recall the awful stench generated by that soma brace. Needing to be in constant contact with my neck, it enabled bacteria to nest, carte blanche, in my sweat. What relief when it had to come off for cleaning me up. Yet, even workers were afraid to remove it to disinfect me, because of the chance of my neck re-breaking. I can easily recall the apprehension in their faces as they performed this delicate procedure.

As my internment at John Wesley Hospital, and subsequently at the Rehab Center, morphed into weeks, and then into months, I learned much about life, and that it was all about suffering. Little things, but to me very big things, had a way of imposing their lessons about survival. More accurately, these small daily encounters with the reality of my utter immobility became tutoring sessions about what I would have to do to mitigate my suffering while surviving. Every situation, every event and its import, was logged in my mental life-or-death manual.

Along with me, three other patients occupied my "quad room." There was a man from Minnesota who had been paralyzed in a snowmobile accident. Another man had a cervical spine injury resulting from an automobile accident, and his head was held in cervical traction to maintain absolute, immovable stability. Since his bony cervical vertebrae, which contained and protected his delicate spinal cord, was broken, the danger was that his cervical bones would re-break, placing him in danger of injuring, or even severing, his spinal cord. That man had to remain on his back, motionless for over ninety days!

Next to me was a paraplegic with a strong upper body, who was able to transfer himself from bed to wheelchair, and back again by means of pulling himself up on a trapeze that hung over his bed. His strength was impressive.

Finally, there was me. Because of my complete inability to move in the slightest way, I was considered a "three-man lift." It was very hard to get three people together at any one time to take me for any studies or evaluations of my condition. I was by far the worst of the lot in my room. I was in such continuous danger of dying that they kept a tracheotomy kit next to my bed, just in case I stopped breathing. My diaphragm barely worked, and my breathing was shallow— a set-up for pneumonia. Several times a day a respiratory therapist would visit in an attempt to try to re-teach me how to breathe. This was common for most everyone after surgery, but mandatory for all quadriplegics, since they are subject to extraordinary breathing difficulties. Ordinarily, one would expect to be in more stable overall condition before major surgery would be attempted. But, it was just because of my tenuous state that surgery was required.

Even now, as I tell my story, having been so routinely close to death, I can easily recall the disgusting odor of the menthol medicine they put into my breathing apparatus to help me cough up phlegm. Breathing this mentholated medicine, drifting along with the flow of clean air, kept me from suffocating. How could I complain? The only alternative to this protocol was to have a tracheotomy, or die.

If this were not bad enough, I learned quite quickly that neither my roommates nor I got any attention immediately upon request. My bedfellows and I soon learned to work as a team. The four of us, when blended together, equaled one person! If any one of us was in need of a nurse, all four of us would turn on our call lights. Then, on the count of three, we would together yell, "Nurse!" *My* "yell" was more of a croak. When one would finally answer our distress call, the one who she attended would not let her leave, but direct her to another roommate after she completed her task. In this way we managed to intimidate the staff into providing us with more than they were willing to give. We were all patients of Dr. Meyer, and I wondered was this the kind of treatment those in his care received? We all learned quickly the truth about this hospital, and talked freely about it. I believe these outbursts saved us from insanity.

One day, after surgery, while lying flat on my back in a neck brace, an aide brought me some food. It was a pork chop with fat marbled all through it. She cut the chop into large chunks and did not trim off the fat. She was oblivious to my weak request that she trim the meat, and instead pushed a hefty portion into my mouth. So fast did she deliver that food to my mouth that I did not have time to chew or swallow, and began to gag. Through a mouthful of meat I mumbled, "Please don't give me so much so fast." Without responding she continued to move the meat into me. I gagged again, then choked and spit out the food. This did not have the effect of waking her to my dilemma. She continued to press on, with a vengeance.

2/11/76 "I have been meeting with Michael on a weekly basis. He does not want to talk about his disability at this time. I feel that we have to let him go at his own pace in terms of talking about this. I think that once he is off the cart and in a wheelchair he will be more open. He has a lot of anxieties and fears at this time that we are trying to help him cope with."

"His range of motion is within normal limits in all extremities. Strength is zero bilaterally in both lower extremities. Shoulder muscles are poor minus. He has no wrist flexion."

"We are working on feeding. He is anxious and very quiet, and seems to be depressed. We are meeting with the family to discuss their concerns and how we can all work with Mike better."

Staff Chart Notes From the Rehabilitation Institute of Chicago

Another day, in February of 1976, after I had been moved to the adjacent Rehabilitation Institute of Chicago to start physical therapy, a similar incident occurred. I was burning up with a 106-degree fever from a bladder infection. Aides packed ice around me over the entire length of my body. I asked one of them for water, because without asking, I found, no one would think to assume I needed it.

When she brought the water, I had to drink quickly so that she could get on with some other duty. I learned to gulp as fast as I could, and would swallow a whole quart all at once. In spite of my eagerness to drink, based on an apprehension that I would get no other opportunity for water, the aide forced me further, by pouring the water into my mouth. She did not seem to care, or even to notice my choking. What could I do?

These frustrations were my hourly attendants, yet at this early point in my handicapped journey it did not occur to me to think in terms of lessons, or what else this could be all about. I could never really turn my head sufficiently toward hopelessness to ask what larger meaning this sad state of affairs had for me. To do so would have been to admit access to some lurking idea that this was all there was. Forever! And, that there was NOT ultimate meaning to it at all. I suppose also that my adolescent mind would not have been able to get itself around the idea anyway, so that I had a kind of natural immunity from such ponderings. Nevertheless, an unformed question regarding a larger purpose was there, cocooned in the deep recesses of my psyche. There it would simmer until ample accumulated suffering prompted it to emerge.

2/26/76 *"Michael exhibits an unusual drive to achieve and thus is afraid to be depressed, dependent, or unproductive. He associates dependency with weakness. He is self-conscious and anxious regarding his disability and is very uncomfortable with the passive-dependent position he is now in. Michael initially will try to control a situation, but once confident, will become warm and interactive."*

"Generally, Michael will not act out or present behavior problems, but may need permission to feel bad about his disability and the ramifications. Once Michael can take a more active role in therapy and his rehabilitation process, he will become more responsive. Contact Dr. Reidy to discuss test results and further reaction to disability. Begin psychotherapy and work closely with the family friend who he trusts."

Chart Notes From the Rehabilitation Institute of Chicago

On the other hand, I harbored a secret rage at the whole state of affairs. *I hate being treated this way. I hate having to be in a condition that permits, even encourages, this insulting and abusive conduct. I would never treat people this way!*

But, had I expressed the outrage I felt at times, they would have defined me as a "bad" patient, intractable, and thrown me out of the hospital. I would have gotten nothing. Like the troubled Hamlet in Shakespeare's famous tragedy, I thought deeply about this dilemma, and a course of action,

"To be, or not to be: That is the question.
Whether it is nobler in mind to suffer the
slings and arrows of outrageous fortune, or
to take arms against a sea of troubles, and
by opposing, end them?"

Although I wanted the latter option, unlike Hamlet, I could not take arms against this sea of troubles, this hospital, these people, this failed body, and end them. Must I then quietly and nobly suffer? No! I had to keep my end goal in mind. Walking. To that end, I sublimated those negativities, and through daydreaming transmuted them into thoughts of recovery. *Maybe there is new research in Russia. Maybe some university laboratory is developing a fix for quadriplegia.* In this way I consoled myself, generated some hope through a kind of benign denial, and maintained a working relationship with the Rehabilitation Institute.

Each day a different member of my family visited me. Since RIC was in downtown Chicago, and they were in the suburbs, it took them more than two hours to make the round-trip journey. Mom came about three or four times a week. Dad about once a week. It was harder for Dad. I knew they could not handle seeing me this way. But, I give him credit for not running away from this whole thing. My sister, Peggy, who was a hairdresser, came every day, at first. She would arrive at the Rehabilitation Institute at four in the afternoon with some sort of real home-cooked food for me!

My brother Jim, who was an eighth grade reading teacher for at-risk kids, would come on Saturdays because he did not want to be there when anyone else was. No one else came on Saturdays anyway. During those visits, Jim and I spent real quality time together. I had him all to myself, and was able to imbibe his wisdom, which otherwise would have been diluted by the presence of more idle chatter. For me, Jim was different than the others in my family. He was my only brother, who had been another male role model, right along with my Dad. Also, emotionally, he was a backup system for me, for I felt that if everyone else deserted me, Jim would still be there.

And, my girlfriend, Jill, appeared almost every night. I lived for her and my family to come each day, because I was so very alone. In addition, seeing them reduced some of my hopelessness about the treatment I was getting. I hated the Institute intensely at that time, because none of what they were doing was focused on making me better or healthier. Rather, we were all inmates in a body prison learning how to accept our condition as final, and we were expected to function as lifelong cripples.

So-called "C" injuries referred to the upper seven sections of the "cervical spine," or bony structure encasing the spinal cord. Injury to any one of them threatened injury to the delicate spinal cord itself. An injury that crashed through any one, or a number of them, would likely injure, or even sever, the spinal cord, rendering the patient paraplegic, quadriplegic, or dead. By far, the most serious spinal cord injury, in which a patient lived, was to be rendered a high C-1 or C-2 quadriplegic. However, just where the injury site was would determine how handicapped the patient would be.

A person with a C-3 injury would be dependent on a ventilator. This was because breathing functions are controlled, or enervated, in the spinal cord, at the third cervical vertebra. Therefore, messages to breathe coming from the brain could not get past the injury site. Hence, no automatic breathing response. In such a person's case, for example, a nurse would have to suction his throat. Without that regular rescue, he would drown in his own saliva. Nor could he ever leave an Institute unless he had someone who could take on that death-defying chore.

A person with a C-4 injury should be able to breathe on her own, but not move her wrist. A C-5 is able to brush her teeth with a wrist cuff attachment. A C-6 is able to do some upper body dressing. A C-7 could perform some lower body dressing using a hook. My own injury was at the C-4 level, and I was nearly insane with the absurdity of it all: the surreal and desperate senselessness of what I witnessed each moment of my waking day. It was only when someone came to see me that a patch of reality, a glimpse of what I once knew, entered my miserable world.

Another apprehension I entertained about the Rehabilitation Institute also worked on me. The Institute operated according to their own brand of a Golden Rule, getting patients to function as well as possible within the limits of their individual injuries. At that time, it was explicitly NOT their role to expect, or help, anyone to go beyond the limitations set by one's medical diagnosis. I was sixteen-years old, and I thought such a policy was absurd. Their mission was not about trying to get me or the other inmates to feel, to move, to walk, but rather, how to adapt to a wheelchair. We called it the "rehab recipe." All activity within the Institute remained within the parameters of that precept. It promoted a fierce competition among the inhabitants of the Institute.

For example, paraplegics would look down on quadriplegics as a predator would look on its prey. A paraplegic could put on clothes. Could push a wheelchair. Could insert suppositories. Could do catheterization. Could transfer to a couch within seconds. Had the use of hands. They were the cream of the crop. And, they knew it. They talked down to those who had even the slightest additional handicap. A C-6 looked down on a C-5, a C-5 looked down on a C-4, and so it went.

Each of us in his or her own layer of prison showed off to the staff, played favorites, tried to get special attention, or worse, belonged to a cripple's gang. Those of us who were quadriplegics felt very inferior. If we were clever enough to make friends with a handicapped person just a notch better off than we were, we were cool. I watched this play out, and I hated it. But I played, so desperate was I for some attention in my God-forsaken world.

As I said, an important measure of a patient's stability at the Rehabilitation Institute was the ability to utilize that damn wheelchair. Within about three weeks of my surgery, the aides, using a three-man lift, placed me for the first time in a wheelchair. The consequence? I felt utterly helpless, and worse off than if I had been lying flat. Rather than sitting up, I was in a semi-reclining position. I felt like Jell-O about to slide off the edge of a tipped plate. I would think, *Oh my God, I hope they don't break my neck again. I'll crumble onto the floor in a heap!*

The aides placed me in this position in a wheelchair for about one hour at a time, gradually building up my tolerance for sitting. Once I was able to sit long enough without getting too fatigued, an important goal of RIC, they would raise the incline angle upwards. I had begun by lying almost flat, and then each week or two they would raise the angle a few degrees. Soon, I was sitting at a seventy-five to eighty degree angle. At eighty degrees, I felt like I was almost sitting straight up. During the early stages, I felt like I would die, expending all my precious energy just to keep my body balanced, and my head and trunk from falling onto my knees. Sometimes I could not hold on and would end up with my head in between my knees. I was a Raggedy Andy again. This would make me dizzy. The nausea was so great that I would decide never to go through such torture again. Nevertheless, I did go through it again, because the therapists told me this was the only way out of the Hospital. Once I could sit, then I would be able to do therapy.

But, what was therapy about? There at RIC, walking was not a goal because medical creed stated that it could not be done. No program was available for it. Although I thought Dr. Meyer was going to "fix" my neck during the surgery, all he was trying to do was stabilize it, so that I would stay alive. The fact is, only three to ten percent of the injured that came into the center ultimately walked. However, in each such case doctors discovered, *upon operating, that the patient had sustained a seriously bruised spinal cord rather than a shattered one.* When the swelling subsided, each patient got better and eventually went home.

Suffering sometimes postponed its deadening grip and took the form of what appeared to be a genuine respite. After Dr. Meyer's operation on me at John Wesley Hospital, and after being at the Rehabilitation Institute for three months, the staff introduced me to hydrotherapy. I was laid flat on a canvas bed frame and lifted into the air, suspended by a Hoyer lift, and then dipped into swirling, hot water in what was known as a Hubbard tank. In the tank my arms would be spread out to the side in the form of a cross. Although the significance of the crucifix positioning was not lost on me, this frequent dunking was a delight, and muted the continuous pain in my body, radiating from my neck and "frozen" shoulders. I began to look forward to it because I could notice some arm movement beginning to occur. Was it possible that these people did know, after all, what they were doing? Then it occurred to me, I had been spontaneously drawn to seek a hot, watery experience in the early moments after the accident as I lay on the ice. Was this the healing experience I had intuitively sought in my psychic distress? Hope surged, I smiled, and life was better again.

Other, less agreeable experiences began accompanying this every-other-day dunking. Staff members would attach my body to overhead pulleys in a canvas frame, and perform a passive range of motion with my arms, forcing them to go back and forth. It hurt, and it did not seem to produce any improvement. Meanwhile, the "who is better" competition continued, even in this setting. "He is lifting more weight than you are." "She is faster than you are in moving her arms." Even the therapists would try to make those with greater disabilities feel more inferior.

"Hey, everyone! Did you know that James, the quad in room 220 is making pizza in the kitchen oven! We have never had a quadriplegic here that could do that."

Those of us who could not move at all felt helpless, overwhelmed, and depressed by the whole notion that someone who could cook pizza would have status. I could not even move my bowels without having a suppository stuck up me. The very senselessness of there being a pecking order in the realms of the damned was revolting. I recalled an old, supposedly humorous adage: "In the land of the blind, the one-eyed man is king!" James was king!

One half of me bought into this performance, and the other half wondered, "Why is there so much competition, and comparing me to those who have had one surgery, or no surgery, or many surgeries, or to those with less serious injuries?" But sadly, I sold out and tried to do well, so that my therapist would brag about me. I never thought of this as possibly being the Institute's motivational technique. They were going about motivating me the wrong way. I wanted to work. I thought, *Who wouldn't want to work? These are the exercises; let's work at them.*

The behavior of the therapists produced the opposite effect on me, and on others, I am sure. Rather than trying to intimidate me, to goad me into competition, I would have much rather had them encourage me, praise me for small successes. Why could these experts not see that this was the formula for success? Maybe the physical and occupational therapists had their own needs to see some sort of progress, in order to justify the tremendous effort they expended in return for such small gains. I eventually decided that the therapists were making overtures to look good to their superiors, to meet their expectations, and they were using us to accomplish this.

As the months passed at the Rehabilitation Institute, and as I became known to them, the staff people would talk to me longer, and I felt more accepted as a person, not just as a cripple, or something less than human. I discovered that, like me, new accident victims who arrived weekly got less attention. I saw them being treated like they were commodities, something that had to be dealt with, but no more. They got the sad and painful treatment I had received in my early days. *So this was it! It wasn't me they didn't like. It was because I had been a novice. I was no longer a novice, a "nubie."* I felt really good about being with the "in group", even if those new kids were on the outside. They could just wait their turn. My recent acceptance felt so good. I almost didn't want to leave this place, due to the hunger I still had for attention and acceptance. What heightened this even more was the fear of going home, a fear that loomed over me as my stay neared its end. Who would take care of me? What would I do with my life? How would I manage to get my needs met? How would I manage to just stay alive and cope with the hours? I was a head perched on a sack of concrete, a Cuckoo marking time in a wooden clock. All I could do was chirp, and I would have to become very clever at it.

To continue the story, skip the Interview and go to the next Chapter.

INTERVIEW

Dr. T.: How long were you at the Rehabilitation Institute? And, how did you improve, overall?

M. S.: I was there from February to June of 1976. During that time I was able to do some mat work, which consisted of attempting to roll by throwing my arms around. I also did some pulley work, which included trying to tug on light weights attached to my wrists by what are called quad cuffs. I did think this work was good, trying to at least build some muscle. Unlike other of my inmates, I asked for extra time on the pulleys because I wanted to gain as much strength as possible.

Dr. T.: You spoke at length about the competition at the Rehabilitation Institute. How those with injuries less serious than your own got more attention, and how fierce the rivalry was for that attention. It would seem that you were transported from being a physical top dog to being an underdog in just an instant. From being one who could perform so much better than others in the athletic world, to one who could not even compete in the handicapped world.

M. S.: Well said, except that underdog could better be expressed as "dead dog." When, at Lutheran General Hospital I would talk to doctors about recovery and walking, they said over and over again to me, "With a spinal cord injury such as you have, you are beating a dead horse." I rose to the level of an underdog when my neck was stabilized enough for rehabilitation at RIC, and much later when I got physical therapy. In the beginning, all I could do was breathe and speak softly. I could not press a call button, feed myself, or anything requiring movement. So, it was a kind of consolation to get to be underdog because there was some small progress. Although I was not happy, I clung to some remote hope.

Dr. T.: What is your explanation of this pecking order dichotomy at the Rehabilitation Institute? That is, isn't everyone living in delusion about who he or she is and what his or her importance is in any of life's settings?

M. S.: In the big picture these ideas are all mirages and illusions. However, in terms of the apparent reality, I can truly say, never take anything for granted. Always appreciate what you have. The lesson for me is that your life as you know it, or more aptly, as you think you know it, can be altered drastically just in one second.

"I am looking for a lot of men who have an infinite capacity to not know what can't be done."

—Henry Ford

7

A BIG SURPRISE

It was a cold and sunny winter day at John Wesley hospital, and an incident occurred that would change the course of my life in every respect, and influence me to the core of my being.

Even though I am now perceived as a quadriplegic, in my core self I am still an athlete, a hockey player. That has not changed. I know hockey. I know the hockey teams. I know the stars, especially those of my own home team, the Chicago Blackhawks. I not only watch their games, but when I was playing for Notre Dame High School, I got to be good at the sport because I watched those Blackhawks play: Stan Mikita, Keith Magnuson, Tony Esposito, Bobby Hull. I studied their moves and from them intuited their strategies. I had in some ways become a Stan, a Keith, a Bobby, all rolled into one.

I would emulate Stan's skating style, for example, which was quick and savvy. Not being a large man, he played with his head, anticipating puck movements, always one step ahead of what might happen next. On the other hand, Bobby Hull was one of the bigger men on the ice. He was powerful, and had a spectacular slap shot that I imitated. Then, with Keith Magnuson, it was his resolve and will to play all-out that inspired me. His intensity was one of his most compelling traits, and I expressed it in my own game.

So, that evening I had been laying motionless on a bed staring at the ceiling when I heard a commotion going on across the room from where I lay. Several people, perhaps a small group, were talking in hushed but excited tones. A sense that something was about to happen germinated in my breast. Then, the commotion began to move in my direction, until people began to appear in my line of sight as I lay flat on my back. What I saw sent a thrill of joy running through me. There, smiling down on me in all his colossal glory, surrounded by a small crowd of devotees, was Keith Magnuson! He was fairly glowing and his ruddy features radiated tremendous energy. Beneath a head of thick red hair was a scarred but handsome face, reflecting the warrior that he was. He had cuts on his hands, and a nose that told a story of battle. His massive frame completely filled out the turtleneck sweater and blue sport jacket he was wearing.

When he spoke, his voice was deep and resonant, carrying the tone of one in command. He first introduced himself to me, and then introduced his companion, Chicago Blackhawks executive chef, Hans Aeschbacher. They had come to see me, Magnuson was saying, and to bring me a belated Christmas gift, a cut of prime rib beef that Chef Hans had cooked up. I was agog. I could barely open my mouth in response. No one spoke, and the silence suspended time, for how long I don't know. Then, without any pretense, Magnuson asked simply and directly, "What do you want to do?"

"I want to walk!"

A broad grin crept over his hovering face, as if the implications of my answer were in some way hoped for, in some way expected. I realized only much later that it was that audacious response, "I want to walk," coming forth from the mouth of a hopeless cripple, that would hook us together for the rest of our lives. Magnuson would proudly tell the story of that encounter to countless audiences as the years unfolded.

Keith Magnuson continued to speak to me in a most charming way, his eloquent words instructing me in a no-nonsense approach to achieving success. He discussed many mind and motivational techniques that would help to keep me going. He described the principles of goal setting, and that he would be behind anything that I would decide to do.

After awhile, Magnuson and Chef Aeschbacher left me, and I was basking in a "holy heaven." It did not matter that on the outside I could not even move a finger up and scratch my nose. I swelled and blossomed within, and the joy I felt was very great indeed.

*   *   *   *   *   *   *   *   *   *

Over the years, Keith Magnuson would stay in touch with me, and we would become good friends. Keith would eventually become the Chicago Blackhawks coach. He would study Bart Starr and Vince Lombardi, and other greats from various sport traditions. He would later come to share those lessons with me:

"Always appreciate people."

"Praise in public—criticize in private."

"A winner never quits—a quitter never wins."

I worshiped these ideas and emulated his example, and had motivational signs placed on the walls in my room, all in keeping with his instructions. Each poster carried only one big, bold word, and read, simply:

DISCIPLINE

CHARACTER

COMMITMENT

I would study these maxims, and use them not only to motivate myself, but I boldly tried to attain what they stood for. I am also aware that it was as much Keith's celebrity status as his high-minded motivation that inspired me. I felt close enough to him to consider myself a member of the Blackhawks family. It was this early inspiration and imprinting on such high concepts and heroes that would bring me to other inspirational, motivational, and behavioral champions who would coach me toward my goal.

* * * * * * * * * *

In about March of 1976, three months after my winter ride to John Wesley, I was given a pass from the Rehabilitation Institute to visit home for a day. With all the misgivings I held, what a marvelous break it turned out to be for me when I left the Institute. I have five sisters and a brother, all older than me, and they all agreed to go through some training in how to deal with my incapacity. My sister Carol, a registered nurse, took on the job of catheterizing me,

Mom and my sister Peg typically collaborating on my nutritional needs. My sister Mary, an executive secretary, my brother Jim, and my sister Janet had the task of inserting suppositories to get my lethargic bowels moving. My sister Joan, an X-ray technician, helped with my personal care, grooming, baths, and turning me in bed. How humiliating it was for me. I would be placed on my side for an hour or more waiting for some movement of my bowels. Mary would have to stay with me as I lay in waiting. Then I was placed in a toilet chair, and more waiting, sometimes up to four hours, before any action occurred. Worse, at least two or three times a week, my bowels would not move, and Mary, wearing a latex glove, would probe me rectally, hoping to stimulate my bowels. Often I would be strapped to a shower chair, and would wait the whole night for that triumphant movement. This was so utterly unacceptable to me that I tried to study what I could do about it. Eventually I learned that working out hard would help overcome the bowel resistance. Without such a good family, I would have literally been "up shit's creek."

With passing time, RIC authorized more home visits, every couple of weeks, and they unfolded in the same way. It was so good to get home, but so humiliating. What would happen when I was finally discharged from the Rehabilitation Institute? Would I be welcomed back home? And what about the neighbors, whose attitudes I feared, imagining all manner of judgments they may be making about me. "Wow, what a freak that neighbor kid is, huh? He should be in a circus."

What about accessibility to the house? Would I need a ramp? What about the bathroom? How would I use it? At the time, my hands were immobile. I could not go anywhere. I could not do anything for myself. But, I hoped that my family would continue to come through, to just welcome me and not abandon me. I hoped with a very great hope.

One event that lifted my spirits, in the spring of 1976, was receiving a pass from RIC to attend the Illinois State high school championship hockey game with my family. Ironically, the two final-ists were my school, Notre Dame, and Glennbrook North, the team we were playing against the night of my injury. I watched from my wheelchair as Notre Dame won the state championship in front of a crowd of thousands. My teammates, in an emotional gesture, hand-ed the championship trophy over the rink barrier, and into my lap. I kept a stiff upper lip as tears flowed from my eyes.

Back at the Institute, I knew kids who didn't have such good families to help them. They were seriously depressed, and did not get passes to go home — ever. Each person in their family had some excuse for not being able to help their wounded brother or sister or child. The sadness was palpable, and we all tacitly agreed not to talk about it at all, but just pretended that everything was okay.

To continue the story, skip the Interview and go to the next Chapter.

INTERVIEW

Dr. T.: When Keith Magnuson visited you at John Wesley Hospital, what was the nature of the inspiration, of the incentive you got from the experience of being with him?

M. S.: First, a radiant confidence flooded me. A glow of strength. I am reminded of the words of Theodore Roosevelt, "Walk softly and carry a big stick." Keith walked and talked softly, and car-ried a big stick, not just the hockey stick. He carried a stick of char-acter strength, of personal confidence. I was nourished by it. That assurance somehow stuck with me. It waned at times, but when Keith and I made contact with each other through the years it got rekindled.

Dr. T.: How did that friendship unfold?

M. S.: After leaving RIC, Keith reached out to me, and we began an enduring relationship. I would see him at fundraisers; we would talk over the phone, always about high-minded topics, about living life well, achieving goals, and how to enhance performance, both on and off the ice. Sometimes we would talk about the Blackhawks and what was going on with them. Years later, Keith would call and want to meet with me, have lunch, and discuss personal problems or issues. At this time he treated me as an equal, and even as a mentor. Occasional articles about our friendship appeared in the sports section of local newspapers, the Chicago Tribune, and Chicago Sun Times.

Dr. T.: Would you recommend that athletes and other well-known and illustrious people visit sick and injured persons?

M. S.: Absolutely. Today especially, athletes and celebrity figures are presented to children on TV, the movies, and commercial endorsements, as role models. Kids and others look up to their idols and take what they say as truth. Children tend to model themselves after celebrity figures. The celebrities should use their status and considerable influence to present high principles to kids, and to appreciate that at least during their public appearances that they are in fact role models, and having a powerful impact on their viewers. Especially in this milieu, they have an opportunity, and a moral obligation, to make the world a better place.

Dr. T: What inspirational work do you do? Do you talk to the injured? The able-bodied? Do you do therapy?

M. S.: The number one inspirational thing I do is show up. If you knew what I had to go through each day, just to make an appearance, you would understand what that contribution is. My life, how I live it, is the motivational work I do. Of course, I do other motivational and inspirational work, speaking, educating children, visiting the sick, teaching companies how to achieve high-minded goals.

Dr. T.: Can you demonstrate how your own inspirational work has had an effect in improving people's lives?

M. S.: Yes. I get letters from other speakers, audience members, and children, who have heard my public speeches. To paraphrase what is regularly repeated to me, "If you can do it Mike, I can do it too." This phrase is so common in those letters that I cannot help but believe good is being done. People are measuring themselves against me, and in doing so gain the insight that they have the potential to achieve their goals as well.

Unfortunately, sometimes others compare themselves to me in a competitive way, and use my success to put themselves down. They see what I have done as beyond their capacity. Their self-image is not as strong as those in the former group. Those people would be well served by working on their personal growth.

Dr. T.: Do you hold resentment for having been one to endure this lifetime of suffering?

M. S.: Yes, to a certain degree. No matter how much I have tried to adjust to the reality of my condition, some resentment remains in me. Ironically, for me there is no one to blame. Resentment is a natural mechanism that comes up when I see others who are free and moving about. I have learned how to repress it, but not to get rid of it. I honestly don't think anyone is totally free of it.

Dr. T.: What is it in particular that sets off this resentment?

M. S.: That's a good question. Probably some level of deep, ongoing and insistent frustration that overrides my efforts at repression. It comes on quickly, a build-up of anger and disappointment that takes over my conscious thinking for a time. It lasts for just a split second — watching someone jump or hop, or even watching someone walk in the mall — and then I put it back where it belongs. Sometimes several weeks pass before it comes up. Sometimes just a few days.

Dr. T.: What techniques, in addition to repression, do you use to keep the rising tide of resentment down?

M. S.: Reality testing. I look inside and examine myself, and reaffirm that I can't do much more than I am doing about it. At that point there is a breakdown of the angry energy, and a return to what might be called a normalcy. Being a psychotherapist, I recently consulted with the mother of a quadriplegic, and her son. After our session the quadriplegic young man, who was twenty-four years old, was a little afraid to come back. He kept asking his Mom, "What can he tell me?" That was his excuse for not coming back. I told her I might just sit with him, and let him be. He needs time to make adjustments in his mind in order to see himself as an acceptable member of society; time to gradually make the transition from victim to a productive member of his community and accept himself at his own level of functioning. Otherwise, he could either shift to a dreamland state where he lives in delusion, or descend into deep depression. He must instead grow into a place of seeing himself as fitting into life. He needs to gradually transform his vision of himself from one that is a closet cripple, a homebody, or a bitter person and a useless member of society, to one that is genuinely accepted by others. This is not an easy road. How much more difficult, then, to achieve a perspective of seeing oneself as an inspiring person BECAUSE of what you have become?

Dr. T.: How is that possible for most people who suffer such severe handicaps? Are you saying that in order to overcome, or at least override the devastating condition of quadriplegia, you must alter your image in some way so as to see yourself as being an inspiration?

M. S.: That would be a very high level psychological function. But, at least some level of self-appreciation that is self-fulfilling must be attained. A basic stage would be someone feeling good about themselves for just getting out of bed. I know some quads that work almost all day with gadgets, tools and other implements just to get up off their bed. My thinking is that I would rather have someone help me with functional issues, getting out of bed, getting dressed, doing my exercises. Then I can focus most of my time and precious energy on my counseling work, and other involvements that are important to me.

"What lies behind us and what lies before us are tiny matters compared to what lies within us."

—**Oliver Wendell Holmes**

8

INTO THE LIGHT

In about June of 1976, I was discharged from the Rehabilitation Institute of Chicago, since they reported that they could do no more for me. By this time I was able to move my arms slightly, and to clearly know my basic needs. Mom and Dad prepared to have me come back to Des Plaines by beginning to build a handicapped accessible addition onto the rear of their home. This was a huge transition and I began to feel another kind of apprehension. Now I would be entirely on their shoulders; at their mercy, as well. I would be both a burden to their way of life, and dependent upon their compassion. I would be shackled to a wheelchair, consigned to a bed. What did I bring to this relationship? To say I was in a dilemma would be an understatement. Sooner or later they would tire of me and my endless cycle of needs, hour after hour, both day and night. I could not fully appreciate this, and the images of helplessness that floated through my mind were sufficiently disturbing that I repressed them. When such vulnerable notions slipped through the cracks in my defenses I turned my attention fiercely toward the business at hand. Get home, and get to work.

During the early months at home, Jill and I drifted apart. Also, I had to get used to the constant attention from family members, whereas before it was from the RIC staff. I could get mad at the staff, but I certainly did not want to do that with my family. So, I became an ambassador, of sorts, trying to soothe their worries about how I was doing. I began to take on, little by little, responsibilities for my care, and my growth as a person.

It would happen that during the next one to two years, all my family members would rally to help me. They would visit, most often in groups. Quite early, I learned that this wasn't helping me. The easy flow of attending to my own daily and nightly needs that I had taken for granted in my short life before the accident had been ripped from my grasp in one horrifying moment during the hockey game.

Now, I had to be on the ball and plan ahead. How was I going to go to the bathroom? Get showered? Brush my teeth? Get dressed? Get food? Eat the food? Get into bed? Turn in bed? Get up in the morning? Shave? Get outside? Use the phone? Scratch my nose? Turn on the TV?

I mentally revisited the surgical treatment at John Wesley, and the physical therapy I had so often complained about at the Rehabilitation Institute of Chicago. It would happen that in the year 2004, a *U.S. News and World Report* survey of hundreds of medical professionals would establish the Rehabilitation Institute of Chicago as "The best Rehabilitation Hospital in America...," for the last "fourteen consecutive years." Regardless of that pre-celebrity quality of RIC's treatment, those early interventions had at least prepared me in many ways for the incalculably altered life I was to lead. But, I no longer had any access to them in any case. I had to think very deeply about this, and take great care to head off any possibility of being left without the means to get those needs met. I needed a plan.

My life was not all about the dreadfulness of quadriplegia. Good things sprung from my situation. After being home for a few months, in November of 1976, almost a year after my accident, Keith Magnuson and Gil Mesa gathered the whole Blackhawks hockey team and organized a fundraiser for me. It would be a roast of Stan Mikita and Bobby Orr, along with Blackhawk coach, Billy Reay, with professional comedians Stu Allen and Sonny Mars doing the honors.

The legendary Bobby Orr, the enigmatic Stan Mikita, the spirited Tony Esposito, and the indomitable Keith Magnuson, along with the Chicago Blackhawks owner and coach Billy Reay all participated in the fundraiser. To this day the image of Billy Reay sporting a colored feather in his cap during the roast comes to mind first. These memories represent some of the abundant sweetness that has blessed my life.

Through this event, we collected enough money to complete the handicapped modification to my parents' home. But, I still needed a plan, which was affirmed by the Dallas Cowboys head coach, Bill Parcells who once said, "To get to any destination worth reaching you better have a road map. You better know where you are going, and how you are going to get there."

So, think deeply I did, and I eventually devised a formula. What that meant for me was that no matter what I believe in, whatever I wanted to achieve, I first had to determine the basic components needed to make the plan work. Secondly, whatever plan I decided upon must be locked in place long enough to germinate, grow, and bear fruit.

What I conceived was audacious. I was going to walk! To that end, I was going to find remarkable teachers, mentors, therapists, and enlist them to guide me to my goal. Whatever it would take to achieve my goal.

Having made my plan, I put it into motion. I would have to wait six years, enduring the slings and arrows of medical disbelief and repression before my ambitious goal actually materialized.

It all began one evening in 1977 when I gathered Mom and Dad, my sisters, my brother, and their families together and asked them a question. Since they were coming to visit me anyway each week, would they be willing to spread their visits out, so that only one person would come each evening to handle my compulsory and awkward evening rituals around bedtime: Eating dinner, brushing my teeth, bathing, urinary and bowel functions, medications, getting me into bed? Happily for me, they did agree, after very little discussion, and the first stage of my plan was in motion. With this agreement I was able to postpone some of the significant basic worries that plagued my young heart and consumed my every thinking minute. Predominately, how was I going to work again, and support myself? And, what kind of a job could I get?

Mom and Dad, having to work for a living, were not able to be involved in my direct care as much as they would have liked. So, my brother, Jim, took care of me in the summer of 1976, and when he returned to school to teach in the fall, my parents hired a nurse, named Millie, to care for my needs Monday through Friday. Then, on weekends, Mom took care of me.

This initial step of my program was to go on for a few years, and worked quite well in that warm familial atmosphere. It was within that welcoming homey ambiance that I was able to install the next stage: My body strategy. Early on, I adhered to the standard medical precept for all quads in my situation: "All real progress would be made during the first eighteen months, and then after that, only small gains would be made, at best." I was on a timeline. I had to get moving, literally! It was well over six months since the accident, and in this year, 1976, I was not just going to gain some movement in my little finger — I was going to "bust my ass" and *walk!* I was ever so hopeful, especially since, in my mind, I had no other option. I was still in denial of the reality that my body could not be bent into healing itself and recovering most, if not all, of the skills I had so recently lost.

Another component in my formula for walking was that I carried a superstar athlete's principle for the success of my plan with me as a talisman. It belonged to the mighty Blackhawk hockey team star, Stan Mikita. The principle played in the background of my consciousness, and it said: *"If you work hard enough and long enough, you will be able to achieve your goal."* It had worked for Stan in his world of hockey. Why would it not work for me in my world of just wanting to walk?

It was by some strange twist of fate, and I cannot believe it was a coincidence, that as a fourteen-year-old varsity hockey player for Notre Dame, I had been given the jersey number 21, Stan Mikita's jersey number! He was my boyhood idol, and Coach Meyer had even nicknamed me "Stosh," the moniker given to Stan by his own team members. I had patterned my play after his play, using the strategies that I had watched so intently on television during many Blackhawks games. More to the point, if this principle worked for athletic skill, why would it not work to repair an athlete's body? The more I worked, the more gains I would get. In time, should I not certainly walk? I still had my doubts, first about myself, and then about who and what might be out there to support me. Family supported me, for sure, to the extent that they could. Doctors did not support me.

* * * * * * * * * *

As more effort-filled days passed during 1977, I came to realize that I needed to have a back-up plan for the daily, sometimes hourly help I required. I discovered that all too often my family, friends, volunteer helpers, and anyone I had come to depend on, needed to change their time slots promised to me. Sometimes helpers would simply forget to be where I so desperately needed them to be.

"I have a concert," one would say.

"I'd like to switch nights with someone else," said another.

Yet a third would beg off due to a family problem, "Sara really needs me tonight."

The extra time commitments were tiring them. Consequently, I would find myself scrambling to generate help from another place. Most of this scrambling took place in my mind, however. How else could I scramble? It was during these trying days that I began to become expert in thinking ahead, to plan for the ever-present future probability that I would be left alone without resources.

As helpers' appointments to assist me were broken more frequently, due largely to no fault of their own, I would find myself alone and begin to obsess. *How will I get to the toilet? How can I take the medicine that keeps my bowels moving, my joints from freezing, my muscles from spasms? How will I lie down? How will I eat?* I became angry. More words played in my head, *They were in it with me. They promised me!*

But, gradually their minds drifted from the necessities of my life. They had their own dramas to attend to. A point came when I mustered the courage to at least talk to my family about this mounting issue. "I have to live with this seven days a week. "Just give me one evening," I cried. I was severely self-absorbed.

Most of the people in my world had begun to cave in to medical-model thinking. Their words played in my head, *You are not going to get better, Mike. The doctors told you this is the way it is.* My thinking was that their commitment to me was too overwhelming for them, and that their readiness to quote medical rhetoric was only in support of their case to withdraw.

* * * * * * * * * *

It is my experience that at least once a month or so, a quadriplegic will awaken during the night and try to move his or her once active legs. This happened to me. What a shock to my system that was. In that reverie before becoming sufficiently awake, I would intend to move my legs, and while that intention was still a viable expectation, I would awaken just enough to realize that my legs would not move! The emotional pain of those episodes is beyond my ability to explain. Sweat. Tears. Fear. Abandonment. Such words represent the tumult of emotions that churned in my viscera.

All quads also worry about what we call an "unscheduled". This represents such things as a catheter leak; loss of bowels; not being able to lie down; a catheter literally blowing up; vomiting food and lying in it; choking. My life now was learning to live within a cloud of unknowing. Even with double-checking, and back-up planning, my body would still outwit and betray me. And I, the talking head on top of the block of cement, would pay an awful price. When something went wrong it spelled misery, humiliation, life or death. Entire days were ruined if one such event occurred. *Take the day, Mike, get help to clean up your pants and then go to bed.* I called it an "anti-quad day" because the forces seemed to be unreasonably stacked against those of us who were cripples.

In spite of all these issues and setbacks, I continued to forge a path to walking. I had gymnastic mats brought in from the local park district facility where I had previously done maintenance work as a high school student. These thick five feet by eight feet pads were where my daily workouts took place. Yet, the word "workouts" is a misnomer, for I was helpless and needed a mover, someone to work me, and the first person who was there to be my engine was a physical therapist named Trudy Vrileink.

Trudy was an experienced and independent forty-something physical therapist from Holland. She had a husband and two daughters living in Glenview, very near Des Plaines. She was blond, big-boned, large breasted, and very set in her ways. It was Trudy's way, or no way. Her patients did not have much to say about their therapy. She would enter for a session and take over.

Mom and Dad had hired Trudy at my behest to take on the task of assisting me in my "walk program." On those mats, along with the ever-present assistance of Trudy, I rolled, tried to do pushups, strained to crawl. I could do none of those things alone, however. Trudy would situate me in positions that resembled someone who was actually moving: doing pushups, doing sit-ups, crawling. Trudy would place me on my stomach, and then pull my knees up under my hips. Then she would position my elbows under my chest, so that I looked like I was a six-month old baby about to take off in a crawl. That, in fact, is what I felt like.

Of course, my motive in taking these postures was to stabilize muscle groups that I would need for my eventual maiden crawl. After months of such passive posing, it became clear that my efforts were futile. I reached impasse after impasse. For example, I could remain in a crawl starting position for five seconds, then by the next week I was able to hold it for ten seconds. But, then in the third week, I was back to only being able to stay on hold for five seconds. This seesaw progress became defeating to me, both emotionally and psychologically. It made me sad. It also spawned in my mind early imperceptible doubts about my formula for walking again.

My relationship with Trudy was one of mutual respect. She acknowledged my proactive attitude and perseverance, and I respected her skills in planning, and isolating muscles that needed to be worked. She helped me in moving my arms, and kept me in great condition in terms of muscle tone. But, she also was disdainful of my healing formula, and disparaging of my expectations of walking. "Spinal cord injuries don't walk!" I resented, and even hated that part of her that rolled over for and even embraced that doctrine; that rhetoric of acceptance that I had gotten from all medical people, hospitals, and rehabilitation centers.

At night, a member of my family would arrive and make the same moves with me that Trudy had made during the day. I thought of being in a kind of football or hockey training camp, with workouts twice a day, five to seven times a week. Days with the professional. Evenings with the family. And yet, from a distance, the absurdity was obvious. Mostly, I was a flesh-colored still-life on a canvas tumbling mat. I felt more like that infant trying to get going, but unlike the infant, the wires connecting my brain to my body had been severed.

In spite of all these limitations, I kept close to me, ironically, another Rehabilitation Institute tenet: "With a good family your chances of success in coming out of troublesome predicaments increases dramatically." That idea staved off many doubts that would have certainly arisen in me. I had such a good family. I had the best chance to overcome the Institute's "predicaments."

To continue the story, skip the Interview and go to the next Chapter.

INTERVIEW

Dr. T.: You created for yourself a formula, a plan to walk. Did your plan work?

M. S.: Yes, because I did finally walk, with my own legs, under my own power. What I failed at, though, was not setting my goals high enough. I was so intent on disproving the doctors' negative pronouncements that I kept myself boxed in. Without realizing it, I had set upon only doing enough to demonstrate for them I could walk. Had I thought outside the box, I could have set the bar much higher, and possibly been a full time walker, rather than just walk for therapy. Further, I could have spent more time in meditation and visualization, and more time living in my own belief system rather than making my work a chore.

The way I explain this in my talks is to tell people that they should reach for a star, since stars are the farthest elements from the earth. If you don't see the stars, and don't then reach for them, you will grasp another closer body, a planet or a moon. Thinking about it, I did get hold of a moon—I walked. I could have shot for a star—developing and living in high-minded values—earlier.

Dr. T.: Do you still believe in planning?

M. S.: I think it is okay to plan, but also to figure into your program all obstacles, and to then just go with the flow and be in the now. As *you* so often say, write into your plan the possibility of failure—then get on with it as if it does not exist.

This acknowledgment of the very real possibility of failure gives it its due, effectively disarming it. Then you can get on with your plan without being covertly harried by its undermining influence.

Dr. T.: You also enlisted teachers, coaches, and mentors, even as you are one yourself today. Do you believe in them? Do you use them?

M. S.: It is always good to have a mentor and to check in with him or her from time to time, in spite of having learned what the mentors teach. Sometimes we need to be reminded, more than informed. You will get from the mentor what his or her philosophy has always been. But that reminder is what we all need. Readers are getting to know those mentors throughout this book.

Dr. T.: "If you work hard enough and long enough, you will be able to achieve your goal," said Stan Mikita. Is this true principle still true for you at some level?

M. S.: I still see much truth in it. But, in addition to working longer and harder, you can also work smarter. There is that old saying, "Hard work beats talent when talent doesn't work hard." I don't know who said that, but it is certainly a hockey player's mentality.

Dr. T.: Although she was a physical therapist, was Trudy's disbelief in your program to eventually walk detrimental to you at the mental stage you were at when she worked with you?

M. S.: Physically speaking, Trudy was right for me at the time. She kept me in great condition, helped me move my arms successfully. But, she was stuck in the medical dogma that people with spinal cord injuries don't walk. That box did not serve me. Perhaps it challenged me in a way that contributed to my determination.

"Never give up."
                                    —**Winston Churchill**

9

LIVING SISYPHUS

Late 1977. Lingering summer days became the shadowed days of fall. The colors and crispness of the season yielded to the encroaching cold and furtively turned gray and dead. My hours, my days, filled with effort and activity, faded into weeks and months. Before I knew it, the frozen winter of my original discontent was upon me, and it was December, 1977. Two years had passed since my accident. In spite of the somber Midwestern skies, and the fact that I had made little physical progress toward walking, I marshaled all my inner resources to exploit the weeks and months ahead. I was still working according to my original plan, and having seen some gains, especially in the area of muscle bulk increase, I forged on. My focus and bravery notwithstanding, the first kinks began to surface in my ironclad healing formula of HARD WORK = WALKING.

Starting in late fall, and carrying over into the winter, I fought depression because I was feeling stuck, confused, and frustrated with my progress. This was so even though I had rejected what the folks at the Rehabilitation Institute of Chicago had recommended I do: accept where I was, get on with life, finish high school (which I had done, from a hospital cart in the rehab center), and go to college, especially since there was government money to do so for people like me. They had proposed a quadriplegic's life to me: "Here is your cushion, your wheelchair, and your catheter; accept your condition and get into college." But I had scorned their advice, and kept plugging along on my mats, youthfully hoping for some glimmer of even a small measurable shift in my body's responses. I also had a second hope: that some new intervention for spinal cord injuries would be discovered. Through the local, Oakton Community College library, Mom and I researched a new enzyme treatment at a Russian Research Institute, but they would not accept me. This was a good thing, because it turned out that the treatment had no real value. Another hope dashed.

Insidiously, in spite of my good fight, the depression began to take root in my brain. To ease it and pacify the nagging idea that I had made a horrible mistake, I enlisted drugs. Alcohol, marijuana, pills. I got these through acquaintances, and through prescriptions. But the gloom only worsened, and so I resorted to blaming others, and especially God, for what had happened to me. I then entertained anger, non-acceptance, and finally suicide. I was belatedly going through several of Dr. Elizabeth Kubler-Ross's stages of grieving: denial, anger, blame, bargaining. But not acceptance. All steps coalesced into one great despair.

I held others responsible for my plight. Certainly, I did not blame myself! The wild dash I had made for the hockey net that night was a familiar move in any player's repertoire of tricks. It was one from which I had often scored. Since it had worked so many times before, and gotten me great cheers, why did it not work then? I hated this paradox with a great hate.

This was my mental state in the winter of 1977 and into 1978. Depression was increasing, hope fading. Suicidal thoughts, recreational drugs, alcohol, denial and depression characterized my life. Others, especially God, were to blame for my circumstances. I had really gotten no closer to getting my body to move, in spite of all the manipulations I had engineered. It was still the dead thing that had lain on the ice two years ago. Although optimism was of vital import to me, it was steadily being relegated to some remote mental outpost that barely registered on the screen of my awareness. I was like the mythical Sisyphus, King of Corinth, rolling that boulder up a hill in Hades over and over again, only to watch it come tumbling back down each time. But, unlike King Sisyphus, my body was the boulder, and it would not even budge.

One day, sitting in my wheelchair more than two years after the accident, I mulled over these imponderables in the cold Illinois winter. With no answers forthcoming, my mind dropped into a reverie. In that zone between waking consciousness and sleep I found myself in the basement of my girlfriend, Jill, many weeks before the fateful hockey game. Images swirled in my head, and I "saw" Jill and me together listening to music. As the album from the rock group "Chicago" played in the background, subtle but disturbing words suggested themselves to me, *You are not going to be around for a long time.* How could I have missed that premonition back then? It had been lost in the happiness and activities of my life.

Eventually, I came out of that reverie, but the experience was disturbing, and left me with a sadness that would not easily disperse. I wondered why I had not recalled that incident until so long afterward. How could I have missed what now seemed to be a clear forewarning? Maybe because of its subtlety? I had never mentioned this feeling to Jill, or anyone else, for that matter.

Regardless of these ghostly musings, and the mounting depression, workouts were what I could do and what I lived for, each waking day. They were the concrete moment-to-moment ingredients in the formula for walking again: the daily and hourly process of working, sweating, and trying harder. That training was almost completely passive in the early months, in that someone had to be there with me to manipulate me. Yet they dissolved into a seamless flow of persistent physical activity that maintained, as well as generated, a kind of proactive and "down-to-business" mindset in me. It would be this attitude that would fuel all the other alternative healing modalities, activities, and interventions I would come to enlist, such as acupuncture, massage, energy healing, biofeedback, and visualization. This particular mind-set generated the inner mental platform upon which I would begin to look at this predicament of mine in whole new ways.

In addition to my evident proactive attitude and behaviors, another secret obsession I carried was about just being healed miraculously. Because no meaningful change came, I was beginning to turn back to God. This was the kind of flip-flop attitude that characterizes this type of predicament. How convenient, since I had no other place to go, but to return home to Father with hat in hand, and beg for mercy.

So, I prayed. And prayed. But, nothing really changed as a result of that either, and an anxiety-laden question appeared to me: *You are basically a good person — why does God not heal you?* I could not dwell on that point too much for fear of having to look at the idea that God did not care. Or that God did not have the power. Or that God did not exist at all.

I had to avoid any such ponderings altogether, since my very life depended upon a God. As time passed without measurable change, however, I again became angry with God. *How much is enough prayer before I get healed?* Maybe I was doing the wrong kind of prayer. Maybe there was some method I did not know about. I prayed the rosary. Was that what God wanted? I prayed the Prayer of St. Francis. *Lord, make me an instrument of thy peace....* Why didn't it work? If God did do miracles, couldn't He cure a spinal cord injury? Seems simple enough.

Alas, I did not know how God worked. My formulations of prayers, my application of austerities beyond the woe I lived in, did not stir heaven. My sad condition was somehow lacking the necessary requirements to get God's attention. *Was a quadriplegic's inability to move his body parts somehow related to his incapacity to move divinity?*

Despite all of these ruminations and feelings of impending doom that lay just below the surface of my everyday existence, life went on and I did make a kind of progress. It was happening however, not on the outside, but on the inside.

To continue the story, skip the Interview and go to the next Chapter.

INTERVIEW

Dr. T.: You blame God. You beg God. You again blame God. What is that about?

M. S.: I was frantically seeking an answer, and not wanting to take full responsibility for my situation. It was about the little boy inside me looking for someone or something to point his finger at.

Dr. T.: While going through your depression, what was going on in your mind that kept you from seeing, let alone owning, your contribution to that fateful accident?

M. S.: It was easier to blame being hit from behind by the offending player than it was to acknowledge that my perfect move, my pet move, had been discovered. I must not have been thinking "outside the box" or I would have sensed that the other players knew what I was up to.

Dr. T.: What do you mean by "thinking outside the box?"

M. S.: For me that means opening one's mind up to take in more data, expanding one's awareness to perceive more than just what is obvious. In my case, I was mired in thinking that my moves were really spectacular, and that no one would intuit what I was going to do on the ice. Not only that, I believed that I was so fast that even if they did figure out what I was up to, no one could catch me anyway. I was speed. I was indestructible. In my speeches to youth groups I spend time at this point to dispel in their young minds, the myth that anyone is indestructible.

Dr. T.: You spoke about going to church earlier. Did not God abandon you? Not answer your prayers? Why do you still have faith in a God? Why is God in your life?

M. S.: Over the years I have learned that there isn't anything else. I have learned that going down on one's knees, so to speak, and begging for help, is an intervention. *It is a treatment.* There isn't any other way to go. If I abandoned being on my knees and just rode the highs of life, those highs would eventually bring me back to my knees once again. So, I have it wired in my head that it is better for me to stay on my knees, or as close as possible to them. That way I don't get so fooled by life's illusions.

"The greatest discovery of my generation is that a human being can alter his life by altering his attitude of mind."

—**William James**

10

MIND POWER

Deep in the gray cold that is February in the Midwest, I lived and plowed forward with my training. Spring, summer, and fall had passed, and it was winter again, of 1978. More than three years had passed, unremarkable from an outsider's view, emotionally stagnant from my insider's spot.

I was still living at home. I worked out with Trudy in the morning. I worked out with family or assistants at night. When I wasn't working out I was watching TV or reading the newspaper. Every once in awhile, I would get to a Blackhawks game, maybe see Keith Magnuson.

One day, my sister Janet spoke to me about an interesting man, a philosopher/psychotherapist who was also a former monk she knew, whose name was Dr. Clarence Trausch. This man was apparently doing some unconventional work with inspiration, motivation, and what he called "applied philosophy," and Janet was quite impressed with him. She had been looking for higher understanding of what my injury was about, and her experiences with him around her own personal growth convinced her that he had the knowledge and perspective to enlighten and help us.

It happened that my sister Peg had also visited him for consultation in her own life, and spoke with the same enthusiasm about him. They both suggested that I might want to talk with him, especially since I was depressed and losing ground in my original optimism. Hearing about him reminded me of my bad experiences at the Rehabilitation Institute of Chicago, so that I was anti any kind of mental intervention. But my Mom got behind my sisters as well, and pushed me over the edge. As a result, they prevailed and made an appointment for me.

"All you have to do is just talk to him," announced Janet.

"Just one meeting," cooed Peg.

What the hell? What could seeing him once hurt? Anything that would make me feel better, since I was in and out of depression.

But, I was no fool. I would retain my reserve. These medical and mental health people were insane. They in no way understood me or my unique set of problems.

My sister Carol drove me to his office in Wheeling, Illinois in a special van that had a wheelchair ramp off the side door. Arriving at his office, I was carrying a load of trepidation in my gut. Carol got the van door slid open, maneuvered me down the lift, and to the office door, where this doctor met us. He was wearing casual, light-colored khaki pants, and a dark sweater. He smiled as he greeted me, and my trepidation softened. In his eyes and face, I saw the same light, the same glow that had manifested in the form of Keith Magnuson. Was it possible that he was my next step in moving forward? It had been years since Magnuson's appearance at John Wesley Hospital, and I very much needed a booster shot of high inspiration.

The first problem was that his office was up a flight of nine very steep stairs. Well, what now? Dr. Trausch offered to pull me up those stairs. The anxiety that germinated in my stomach sprouted. I could just see myself in my mind, halfway up those stairs, him letting go, and me tumbling down to my death, or great injury, helpless to do anything about it. Carol told him that he would have to get behind the wheelchair, and pull and lift me in it up those stairs backwards. Without hesitation he grabbed the handles on the back of the chair and began an ascent. Halfway up the stairs, I could sense he knew what he was doing. Strong biceps. *I wonder if he has strong medicine as well.*

We arrived in his office at the top of those stairs and Carol left us alone. I was in a bright, airy room with loads of windows looking out to his backyard lawn. In the room were bookshelves loaded with volumes, and a desk and chair. He never went behind the desk, but took a seat just inches from where I sat in my wheelchair, almost knee-to-knee. As he gazed at me with calm, penetrating eyes, I became aware of my apprehension — that he knew what was inside me. I was afraid that he would uncover things that I did not know about myself. I had been poisoned by the therapists and psychologists I had in RIC and in the subsequent family therapy. I was afraid that he would read me the doom and gloom rhetoric that was rehab's fare, and would put me in another medical peg and leave me there.

As we gradually became acquainted, he talked to me and questioned me in this calming, confident voice, and I had the thought that maybe this would work! Doctors and therapists that I had previously encountered had just pushed information down my throat. They defined me as having something wrong. They made me feel guilty for the events around the accident. I had been brainwashed into believing that I had done something wrong. With the family pushing therapy so much, I was carrying a load of guilt that I had not only been responsible for the accident, but also for how the lives of my Dad and Mom, brother and sisters had all changed. And, that I could somehow have prevented this life of gloom I now lived.

Dr. Trausch actually listened to me. He treated me like my accident was an event rather than an intention. Suggested that although we have free will, many circumstances are out of our conscious control. This was good! I did not at the time know it, but this was the beginning of my journey into the realms of philosophy and wisdom.

Our session ended and again, he lowered me in my wheelchair gently down the flight of stairs we had ascended earlier. We said some parting words, and as I headed home with Carol, I reflected on other words we had shared: that this time together was confidential; that any further sessions were entirely up to me — my choice; that we would dialogue and learn and grow together. I felt that I was with a friend and was so happily enchanted that I initially began to see him twice a week. He was exciting, motivating, and was presenting ideas I had never even thought existed. I learned what genuine empathy was!

As our sessions progressed, Dr. Trausch proved to be a very bright young man, well versed on almost everything, highly motivated, a positive thinker expressing confidence every moment. He reminded me of the boxer Mohammad Ali who, although he could knock you out with one commanding punch, rather chose to dance, to bob and weave, to gracefully float across the ring. He would take you to the edge of possibility, and then bring you back to safety. He stayed with me, moving me around the ring of creative possibilities, so to speak. It was a delight to watch him weave symbolism and metaphor into his lessons, and actually make me enjoy not only learning, but to see discipline and risk and effort in a whole new light. I don't know if Dr. Trausch knocked his clients into enlightenment, but he had the power to do it.

More time passed, and he worked with me at what he called a psychological "threshold level," meaning that he would not push me emotionally beyond where I could go, or was willing to go. Equally, he told me that he would challenge me regularly to get beyond where I was, to approach the borders of my ability, and that this would include all the arenas, thinking, feeling, and movement.

He used a biofeedback machine called the temperature trainer to demonstrate to me how through the use of my mind, I could raise and lower my temperature according to my intentions. He used a biofeedback machine called the dermograph to demonstrate to me that every thought I had, and its quality and intensity, would have an effect in my body in terms of blood flow, heart rate, blood pressure, body temperature, feelings of tension, stress, or wellbeing. He used a machine called the myograph to demonstrate to me that through mental intention, I could make muscles move, even though that movement was not pronounced enough to be seen with the eyes. The machines would light up and respond, audibly and visually, when I was successful in *intending* to move. This gave me previously unseen hope that I would eventually see them stir.

He taught me about intention and how to exercise my will. One way he did this was by crafting incrementally difficult intention exercises for me to practice. He ushered me into crafted visualizations and guided imagery that spoke volumes to my subconscious mind, training it to assist in a unique and powerful way in carrying out my conscious intentions. He introduced me to the notion that the signals my brain could no longer send to my body because the spinal cord wire was crushed, could be transmitted from my mind through another medium, just as voices and pictures could in modern times be transmitted through the medium of space to waiting radios and televisions.

He asked that I suspend my doubt and disbelief, and taught me principles that blended both spiritual faith and quantum physics in such a way that they complemented and supported each other.

With my quadriceps connected to the myograph, he challenged me in various ways to use my will to move my body. At first, no movement occurred at all. But, with willpower built through the marriage of both imagery and intention, the time came when the myograph signaled movement in my quadriceps even though I could visually see nothing at all. It would be such early commanding proofs that formed the motivational basis of my plan to rise, and walk.

How could I resist? In light of my desperation and long search for an answer, these ideas made so much sense to me. This was fabulous. But, Dr. Trausch cautioned me, these ideas were not easily understood or accepted in conventional medical-model thinking. He told me that the medical community's disbelief alone was enough to create the kind of insidious doubt that would inhibit my building faith and willpower. He warned me to behave as if the principles I was being taught were true, but not to set any part of my heart on a final goal. Rather than spend all my energy in attaining my goal to walk one day, in the future I should bring genuine meaning to my life through appreciating the process itself, in the present moment. That is, whether I ever walked or not, ***I WAS TO GAIN MY SATISFACTION FROM THE IDEA THAT I WAS BEHAVING AS BEST I COULD.*** These ideas helped bring my confidence back. He had infused my spirit of wonder and promise with his presence and skill, and I was on a path. I was moving. I was growing, and it felt good.

Eventually, we also did psychotherapy, which helped me cope with the state of immobility I lived in, the ever-lurking depression, the embarrassment, the weariness. He taught me to cast my intention out ahead of where I was, to a place I envisioned going, and then visualize myself growing into it. He taught me to constantly push my boundaries even though it did not at first make sense or feel good. He taught me many growth and healing formulas for body, mind, and soul alike, such as various kinds of meditation, Command Therapy, and Surrender Breathing, and we practiced them each week. In meditation training, for example, I learned how to discipline my mind like a mental martial artist. With that exercise I built a powerful concentration, and an ability to focus in such a way that I could alter my relationship with pain.

"Extend your mental boundaries beyond the threshold of your ability to move. See and feel yourself at that threshold, and make the next small movement." And, "Since you cannot quite grasp this ball, picture yourself now, in vivid color taking hold of it. Reach out. Reach out!"

What in the world is he talking about? I thought at the time. I can't grasp a ball! You don't know the limits of these fingers. But he knew the *psychological effects* of his challenges: that when I would see some success, the thrill of it and the psychic charge it generated within me would propel me into the next threshold of growth.

The progress I made during my initial months with Dr. Trausch was mostly on the inside. But small, initial measurable changes appeared, especially through the eagle eyes of the dermograph, and in subtle but definite changes in my outlook on life. The earlier feelings of impending doom that lay just below the surface of my everyday existence began to scatter, and I began, quite unconsciously, to prepare myself for what was to come.

To continue the story, skip the Interview and go to the next Chapter.

INTERVIEW

Dr. T.: What is it about what I was teaching that caught your attention?

M. S.: Your clever ideas, insightfulness, and your ability to empathize. I needed understanding, and to have someone get inside my head, discover what was true at my core, and not let me off the hot seat about what I needed to face and deal with.

Dr. T.: Today, what is the core lesson, or lessons, that you took from those years together with me that you still utilize to fuel your life?

M. S.: I got that one always has to be a psychologist, of sorts, to acquire and maintain an awareness of people's motivation — why they behave the way they do. This basic knowledge must be kept in mind in all dealings with people. Handicapped people should look into taking a Dale Carnegie course just to acquire a little of the ability to enter people's psychic space, and to understand what they are about, in addition to simply raising their confidence level. Knowing something about what motivates people is a way of taking care of myself, to reduce the chances of being mistreated. Such knowledge translates into an effective living skill.

This, again, reminds me of the Four P's formula, that prescription for achieving happiness, which is discussed in the back of this book.

Dr. T.: Tell us about any doubts you had about these lessons, and the Four P's principles in early years. As you look back, did you embrace this all as it was given to you? These lessons are high philosophy and even today are not common knowledge.

M. S.: Sure, I suffered with enormous doubts. But, I continued to learn and try to absorb and practice what I was taught. Each lesson was presented in a different way, and as understanding increased, doubt would erode away.

Here is one example. It is a common human inclination to judge others at face value. To criticize someone for having green hair, or for ignoring you. But, I learned how to look deeper, to look inside others, using skills relating to intention, attention, and perception, and thereby discover that such people are not basically different from me at all, and that they have motives that make sense to them. In this way, wisdom overpowered the doubt and I grew with each passing day. I still keep discovering and rediscovering new meaning in so many such principles.

Here is another. Take kindness. Many people are not kind to the handicapped. Why should handicapped people be kind toward them? Yet, I have found that in order to survive I needed to be kind. It was a necessity. Then, as I learned the more profound lessons of kindness, I understood that virtue more deeply, and realized that even if I did not HAVE to be kind, the virtue is valuable in and of itself because of the rewards it brings. Kindness is, truly, its own reward. But I could only learn this through the process of living this life I live.

Dr. T.: What advice would you give a quadriplegic about how to use mind power to his or her best advantage? How about how to handle the skepticism about ever walking, ever moving, that you encountered?

M. S.: The best advice I could give is for them to call you or me and get input, get guidance. Go to a coach, a guru who has been there and knows the ways to handle these inevitable situations. That is what I did with my physical disability, and eventually, my psychospiritual needs. That is what you did with your quest for truth. That is why we have successful lives, happy lives in spite of the nonstop trials that are presented to us.

Dr. T.: Throughout your journey, in addition to praying, you learned to meditate. Speak about that process.

M. S.: Studying with your Center, at the time it was the Institute for Metaphysical Research, I attended private and group basic instruction sessions with you, and did a lot of homework, which entailed much practice and fortitude in the early years. Although it was all new to me at the time, I continued to practice on my own, and it began to work for me. Since my body did not move then, it made good sense to use my mind to the fullest. Meditation training awakened me to problem-solving, building inner power to get the necessities of life, as well as to center myself and grow peace of mind. The silence and solitude inherent in meditation practice pulled me on toward a higher inner source of grace and calm.

Dr. T.: Do you teach those meditative mind skills to your clients today?

M. S.: Yes, at an introductory level.

Dr. T.: How do meditation skills contribute to problem-solving for you?

M. S.: In meditation, you can project your problem up onto the screen of your mind, visualize it clearly, and ask for help from a higher power. Often, in a quiet, deeply centered space, you can get very clear answers. Such success takes some practice, however.

Dr. T.: You were raised Roman Catholic, as I was. How does this meditation practice square with your religion, and your family?

M. S.: Our family was disrupted by the accident I had, and we all sought and tried out different solutions to deal with it. With that family trauma, we all took a different look at religion. The question raised for us was, "Why would such a devastating event happen to an altar boy — to 'Mikey?'" There were no clear answers from our church. We all began to search, and meditation was there to provide some deeper answers, along with consolation. Many of the answers that emerged are sprinkled throughout this book, hiding between the lines of my responses to life's challenges.

I must state that the Catholic church does, in fact, include meditation in its spiritual arsenal, but many Catholics are not aware of it.

Sitting in mass, going to a devotional service, or receiving a sacrament all include quiet reflection and sometimes deeper prayer. As the renowned Catholic monk, Thomas Merton, author of *The Seven Story Mountain*, said, "Meditation is the best kept secret in the Catholic church." I like to think of meditation as the last stage of prayer.

Speak your truth quietly and clearly, and listen to others, even the dull and the ignorant; they too have their stories.

—Desiderata

11

UNDERMINING INFLUENCES

This good relationship with Dr. Trausch was working, and after several months, I was seeing some progress. Mainly, beyond my body, my attitude was better. The ideas that were germinating power in me were seeping out in my conversations and behaviors with others. But, as my enthusiasm grew, my friends began to express doubts and even skepticism. Even worse, they discounted my fervor, gave little credit to the quirky ideas that I was embracing, and wrote off as unreasonable what I was growing to live for. They felt I was setting myself up for trouble. Disappointment.

My friends, bless their hearts, were reflecting their own entrenchment in the realms of the mundane world of the commonplace, of the medical model of how things worked, and not thinking outside the box. They did not, could not, understand what was happening in my body and my heart. The medical profession and my family had saved my life, and now they left me in peril of a lifetime lying in the conformist bed of Procrustes. You may recall that the mythical Procrustes, son of Poseidon in Greek mythology, waylaid travelers and force-fitted them into his one-sized bed by stretching, or cutting off, their legs. Unlike victims of Procrustes, my legs were not cut off or stretched. They were dead.

The experiences I was having, however, would translate into the possibility that someday my legs would move. The genuine possibility of walking was germinating in me, and it was nourished regularly by the ideas and enthusiasm flowing from the experiences in working with Dr. Trausch. He was to me a confidence-builder and friend in the beginning, and then I began to incorporate his unconventional ideas about what the mind could do for the body into my belief system. He taught me to travel beyond my programmed thinking: outside my own box!

Even though these exciting possibilities thrilled me, and my family and friends supported me, encouraged me, and saw to it that I got where I needed to go, they still saw me as a dreamer. I became known as "the rainbow-chaser." This unkind label hurt me. Was I looking for a pot of gold?

But, in spite of this label, I continued on for the next year with Dr. Trausch, and the subtle movements I was seeing in various muscles through the sensitive eye of the biofeedback machines and Dr. Trausch's direction would eventually provide me with the courage to approach an orthopedic physician with a request for leg braces.

Also, because of the progress in my inner confidence-building, will-building, and mental focus work with Dr. Trausch, and my outer work with my physical therapist Trudy Vrileink, I was now making visits to Lutheran General Hospital, the place where my medical quagmire had begun, and being placed on a tilt board mechanism. This was an electric contraption that Trudy had requested for me as a backup system, in case she became unavailable.

At home, I had begun to stand some seconds in a walker, with family members helping me, bracing my body and each arm. My body was actually bearing weight, in spite of having been warned by doctors that such an attempt might break my bones. The earlier and unseen movements of leg muscles, magnified through the agency of biofeedback, were translating into movement. He had guided me to new thresholds; aided me in repeatedly visualizing the crossing of new physical boundaries. We would do this repeatedly. And, as we did so, I was increasingly using the encouragement and inspiration that germinated in my heart to make more attempts to actually manifest the unthinkable things I was seeing in my mind.

Not only was this inner inspiration fostering outer action, but also the guided imagery and guided meditations brought me an increasing sense of peace. I was gradually reaching places where my own disturbing thoughts, my quadriplegia, the medical restrictions, the family issues would not bother me.

Previously, I would never have taken measures to stand up for myself. I would never have reconfigured my circumstances in my mind, so that I could conceive of the small but relentless steps. I would never have begun to think outside the box. I was learning how to break life's ordinary experiences into meaningful bits of information that were powerful to me. One of the ideas that propelled me when in deep meditation was "I have more motivation in my little finger than most people have in their whole body." That idea awakened me! If I was thinking and doing all these things, how could I continue to feel bad about myself? I was awakening to a new way of defining my circumstances and myself. I now lived in the realm of possibilities. *I CAN BE MORE!* And, I was proving it to myself.

Naturally, my next big challenge was standing on my own. I needed leg braces. My thinking was, "If only I could get some support, I could stand alone." I had been practicing standing with a walker. Two people would hold me up, one would hold my ass, and another would push my knees into a locking position; and I would try to grip the walker with my hands as I stood there. Even though there was no movement, this was an exercise. The expectation was that my legs, my quadriceps, would grow some muscle. And, that the standing, of itself, represented my passionate intention that I would eventually be able to stand alone. It was my body being placed in the position I wanted it to conform to. It was optimism. It was anticipation. I did a lot of this and hoped it did not disappoint me. I could do very much with hope. It was providing me with an endless stream of energy.

This concentrated labor eventually brought me to the place where I believed I needed leg braces. I had talked my way into progress that I had not yet made. But, those projected ideas became the goals that I worked toward and, to some extent, obtained. In February 1979 I contacted Dr. Tom Fahey, a tall, handsome and intimidating man who spoke with well-crafted words. He was touted as the up-and-coming star of the highly acclaimed Fahey Medical Center in suburban Chicago. I was suspicious of him, as I had been of Dr. Trausch. Yet, he was the man that could prescribe the braces I sought.

When Dr. Fahey saw me in the wheelchair, looked at my X-rays, and read my history, he said to me, "This would be like putting a rag doll into a lead suit." This demeaning prognosis, coming from a medical doctor, was a blow to my confidence. He was oblivious of the yearning to move that smoldered within me. I mustered the reservoir of inspiration and motivation I had accumulated over the past year and said to him, "Let me show you what I can do." With my Dad present, and my sister Carol and my nurse, Pat Drews, on either side of me, I rose from my wheelchair and stood before him. He stared at me for a long time, expressionless and not budging. Then he turned abruptly, went to his desk, and wrote out a prescription for the braces. I sat down, turned, and wheeled out of his office, a skill I was still refining, while my Dad spoke to him in hushed tones. Within minutes, upon Dad's arrival at the van, he reported to Pat, Carol, and me the content of his and Dr. Fahey's private conversation. Dr. Fahey had said: "The boy has tremendous spirit, and that is why I am writing the prescription; but he will never walk again."

Four years later, in 1983, I would go back to that very same room and see Dr. Fahey again, only this time under vastly different circumstances! Then, Dr. Fahey would see for himself what a teen's indomitable spirit could do.

The route to this future event in Dr. Tom Fahey's office was an arduous one. Did I say arduous? Let me rephrase that. The route was punishing. I had taken up the gauntlet. Looking back, he was simply fixated on traditional medical protocol. Nevertheless, my gloves were now off: I was on a path to fake out not just physicians, but the world.

To continue the story, skip the Interview and go to the next Chapter.

INTERVIEW

Dr. T.: How much of your encounter with Dr. Fahey was responsible for powering your motivation to walk?

M. S.: Very little. I did not hold any hard feelings against what Dr. Fahey said. He represented the traditional medical establishment. He was, in fact, a kind man to give me those braces. So, I look back upon him in appreciation, because I already knew who I was, and where I was going.

Dr. T.: Do you understand all of our work together differently now, than you did in the beginning?

M. S.: Yes. Now I understand it as a total process. I needed lessons in the beginning to deal with what was happening to me physically, emotionally, and mentally. It is only if life stings you enough that you will you seek answers. As time passed, however, I grew into the truths I had learned, and was able to face the hand that life dealt me with more presence.

Dr. T.: You seem to have been very, very hopeful about your goals and the positive outcome of your endeavors to walk. How do you look back on that hope now?

M. S.: I believe I would do it all over again, the same way. The perspective I held, and the choices I made, motivated me to get out of bed every day. If you don't have a strong purpose in life it is difficult to rise each morning, let alone do your job. It was the larger goal of ultimately walking that kept me going with such intensity, rather than any one of the smaller motivators that are part of one's daily existence.

As I now say in my motivational talks to sales audiences, on your down days, your larger purpose in life carries you through the smaller trials. For example, when a wise business manager must deal with an employee whose production is falling off, he or she will focus on the employee's goals and aspirations more than the poor production. Eventually your major purpose — what brings meaning to you — will pull you back toward your center, keep you going, and get production back on track.

"If you have faith and do not doubt at all, not only will you do what I have done to the fig tree, but even if you say to this mountain, 'Be pulled up and thrown into the sea,' it will be done."

—**Matt. 21:21**

12

DIVINE
INTERVENTIONS

It was November of 1980. I was twenty-one years old, living at home, and taking some college correspondence classes at Loyola University. I was studying psychology and criminal justice. I did not have any special goals around them, but just liked the subjects. It kept the people around me happy, because they could say I was doing college work. Along the way, I had had several medical setbacks, mainly urinary tract infections. Also, friends were mostly gone, off to college and other pursuits, and I was at home, alone, and somewhat insignificant.

Mom, always searching for new treatments, found Barbara

Devine, a student of sports training. She was using an electronic device called the Myoflex on athletes to enhance their performance. The electrical stimulation fostered communication among neurons and helped build muscle tissue. Ironically, in the medical field, it had been developed and used as an alternative to electro-convulsive, or shock therapy. For neurological disorders, however, it stimulated the central nervous system and the autonomic nervous system, promoting collateral circulation around damaged tissue in the spinal cord. I was skeptical, but agreed to a meeting with Barbara Devine because we had gotten good feedback about her from the parents of another spinal cord injury patient in our city who had used the device.

I arranged to visit this young man's home and to meet Barbara Devine there. Accompanied by Mom, Dad, and my sister Carol, my first meeting with her was fascinating. She was a stern but youthful forty-something woman who was also intimidating, just as Dr. Trausch and Dr. Fahey had been. Brunette hair styled up, she was dressed in an informal suit, and carried herself with grace and elegance. In spite of her seriously professional appearance, she demonstrated an unexpected kindness. Her depth of knowledge of spinal cord injuries was simply amazing. I thought I had known about everything in that category by now, but she sailed beyond the knowledge my entire family had heard or read about, regarding such injuries. When she talked about spinal injury, she overwhelmed me with her expertise, speaking rapidly and comprehensively, pouring out a steady stream of facts. She was like a grand and skilled movie star who knew her subject and her lines well, and astonished her fans.

During our visit, Barbara put me on the Myoflex to do an experiment. She placed one pad on my spinal cord, and the other pad on one of my legs. As the machine began to hum, its internal fans cooling unseen transistors, my quadriceps and hamstring began to flex and throb. I immediately became excited, but held on tight to my skepticism. Then she placed the pads over my kidneys, liver, and large intestines and did a stimulation treatment. I did not feel very much, but when I got home later that day, I had a bowel movement without any suppository! Until then, suppositories were a regular, intimate part of my daily routine. The idea of not having some-one—my sister, my Mom, my brother—have to stick their finger up my butt was a whole world of change. "We are buying that machine," I said. Most unfortunately, however, my insurance company would not pay for it.

What was I to do? Enter Gill Mesa, a retired national Boy Scout leader, along with Keith Magnuson, with whom I had kept an ongoing relationship. Together with Dick Cronin, a family friend, they organized a series of fundraisers. One of the fundraisers was held at St. Mary's Church in Des Plaines. Mom, Dad, my brother and sisters, and many other supporters were there to help. But the cost of the Myoflex was over $2000, and we still had not raised that kind of money. But then, after the fundraisers, the St. Mary's Parish Women's Guild got wind of what I needed and took the reins. They organized a country hoedown through the church. Everyone I knew came, and I was the center of attention, becoming more and more positive with each passing hour. We raised enough to pay for the Myoflex, and some left over to cover some of Barbara Divine's traveling expenses.

By the end of February 1981 we had accumulated sufficient money, and contacted Barbara Devine to order a Myoflex. Then I arranged for her to work with me. She created specific treatments for my various muscle configurations, and applied progressive stimulation, gradually increasing the duration and intensity. Watching and listening to her, was inspiring. Her knowledge of spinal cord/muscle enervation was colossal.

I learned during the course of these treatments, which took place about five to seven times a week, that Barbara had been hit by a car as a child, and was paralyzed for a time. Her claim to fame was the numerous operations she had endured before she was able to walk. I liked Barbara and her story, and she inspired me constantly, telling me of her seemingly endless mental frustrations, and of what it was like trying to walk again: the pain, the persistence, the tenacity of her will to walk.

Barbara was also schooled in nutrition, when good nutrition and good food as valid contributors to healing were considered unthinkable and laughed at. She coaxed me into taking a class to study vitamins, supplements and diet, and I eventually got a certificate in nutrition. All of this positive activity would support my inner mind as well as the outer exercise I was doing, to promote greater muscle mass and better connections between the neurons.

I worked with Barbara until 1984, and looked forward to our sessions in the same way I did with Dr. Trausch. Barbara always held the end goal in mind, which was to walk again. She had a progressive plan. It seemed ridiculous at the time to everyone except me, because helpers had to move my legs for me. So much work did Barbara and I do that my legs would often swell up, and I would cry and take pain medication, sometimes sleeping only an hour at night. My legs would jump up and down. I was like an infant, learning to walk for the very first time.

Evidently, however, the neurons were making connections. I recall two statements made by the renowned athlete, and former head coach of the Green Bay Packers, Vince Lombardi. I frequently seek solace in his words, "The harder you work, the harder it is to give up," and "The greatest accomplishment is not in never falling, but in rising again once you have fallen."

It is this kind of inspiration, I am convinced, that gradually led to my being able to lift my leg while in a standing position, inside the parallel bars!

With great effort, I would lift one leg, put it down, and put weight on it. Then, I would do the same with the other leg. While I was focusing so intently on my lower extremities, I was also making gains in the use of my arms. I was consistently lifting wrist weights to strengthen my arms and my upper body.

In these activities, Barbara Devine drove me relentlessly, like I was some great athlete preparing for the 1982 Olympics. Many times I hated her down to my very core, and wished that she would leave town! In the end, however, I listened with great respect and tried to carry out all her orders.

The outcome? Although my whole body kept resisting, I was walking! Anticipation, which over the years had settled into my psyche as a pallid and stagnant state, was at once justified and rewarded. The biggest breakthrough came at one o'clock on June 11, 1982, when I was able to walk the entire length of the parallel bars.

Even though I actually walked, within me at the same time I also had an overwhelming urge to sit down. Being in the wheelchair had become my way of moving through life, and represented a very real, entrenched security. Now I was challenging that security. I was risking approaching what had become, for my mind and senses, the unknown. To actually make self-propelled motion under my willpower was a formidable barrier to cross.

On that day, after taking that first, real walk, I sat down in my chair, rested, and broke out a bottle of champagne. Mom, Dad, Pat Drews, my sisters Carol and Peg, and Barbara all toasted each other. I was triumphant. I was scared. I was exhausted.

Two months later, the same crowd went outside to the same front yard sidewalk that I had walked confidently and easily down almost seven years earlier to play in a hockey game against Glenbrook North. With great effort that day I would again walk the eight-foot length of sidewalk with just one person holding my hand. No braces, no parallel bars. No doctors. As far as we knew, this had never been done before by a chronic quadriplegic. Barbara Devine, who was there, would later write:

"Six and one-half years of work, blood, sweat and tears have most certainly paid off. Mike took six to eight consecutive steps on the sidewalk today. It is what we have worked for, prayed for, cursed for, and cried for. Only Mike could have done this. I thank God for what happened today, and for the privilege of working with Mike Schwass."

What led to this amazing and much visualized achievement were the months of excruciating effort of trying and trying to get out of my wheelchair. Barbara's tact was to get me out on the lawn in my wheelchair, and coach me in preparing to get up. Each step was delineated: "Put hands on armrest. Lean forward. Strain to move out." This was something ludicrous to ask a quadriplegic to do. I would try. Try again. Then fall. She would let me fall. My helpers who worked with me day in and day out — Tommy, Mike, Barb, Pat, Karen, Joel, and so many others — would see me falling. Hired helpers had become an important part of my arsenal of daily supporters. It was difficult for them, as well as for me. But they, too, trusted this "Devine woman" and what she had to say.

"Let him fall. Let him fall!" She would shout, as the helpers restrained themselves, consternation and pity on their faces. I would cry, sweating, grimy, snot dripping from my nose, lying helpless on the dirt. The helpers would get me up again, position me in the chair, and I would begin the same process over again. Going through my mind was: *How can you be so unfeeling, Barbara? You must have experienced this yourself! Why would you put me through this?*

However, Barbara was the experienced drill instructor. I was her boot camp recruit. This particular exercise had gone on for about five months. And, what did this do for me? I became able to push myself out of that wheelchair and reach for the parallel bars, or someone's hand, and take some steps. A huge gain. A long road. Watch out Sisyphus!

As I reflect back on my years and experiences with Keith Magnuson, Dr. Clarence Trausch, and Barbara Devine, I have warm and varied memories. They were different in many ways, but similar in other ways, as well. Although I seldom saw Keith Magnuson during my time with Dr. Trausch and Barbara Devine, we talked on the phone occasionally. We discussed school, public speaking, motivation, hockey, and we would exchange ideas as if we were colleagues. I would inspire him because I wasn't quitting. He would inspire me because of his celebrity status and persevering friendship. He generated an indomitable faith in me, and a will to match, teaching me the great human values of compassion and fortitude, and modeling them, to boot. I felt I was near enough to him to be considered a Blackhawk.

Similarly, Dr. Trausch inspired me from within, enlisting my mind, empowering my will with mysterious truth, and forging deep psychoneurochemical connections in preparing me for the first steps in what was for the world an impossible endeavor. Armed with his knowledge and wisdom, I had become ready to take the next step and enlist my inner power in the service of my muscles.

Barbara Devine was that next step in manifesting my goal, who inspired me from without, infusing me with her indomitable perseverance, and recruiting my body and already-prepared will, to actually employ those very impossible movements. Barbara Devine coached me through the territory with a confidence that was palpable. With her, the neurons and muscles worked together to move me, to walk me. I was a walking quadriplegic.

To continue the story, skip the Interview and go to the next Chapter.

INTERVIEW

Dr. T.: You have said: "I inspired Keith by my not quitting; he inspired me by his persevering friendship and celebrity status."

What is it about not quitting, even though no progress is made, that is so compelling, so attractive for onlookers?

M. S.: I think perseverance is compelling because at some point in life everyone has had their face in the mud, and they can identify with the fact they eventually came out, or were lifted out, of it. They can look back and see that not giving up, in the end, paid off. Being entranced by someone's heroic perseverance is a product of what they themselves have already experienced at some level. Looking back on it, for me not quitting, not giving up, was certainly nobler than any other option.

Dr. T.: You had studied long with me, and longer with Barbara Devine. What were you thinking you had accomplished?

M. S.: I knew I had accomplished something great in actually walking upright, but I still had it in my head that I needed to walk independently, maintaining my balance without any external support. I also longed to do other things, like kicking a ball, catching a ball, bending up and down.

Dr. T.: Did you think that you were on your way?

M. S.: I knew that if I had accomplished walking, I could do even greater things. That seemed a certainty. I hear the commanding words of Jesus playing in my head, "Pick up your pallet and walk." But, whatever I had achieved, it was never enough. I didn't have an end goal, because I didn't know how high the sky was, what my limit was. It was a matter of finding the right trainer that could take me to the next level. I did figure that I would never be perfectly normal; but at the same time I was calculating that I could reroute more of my brain messages around the damaged portion of the spinal cord, or piggyback mental messages on radio waves. Something unseen such as this had taken place in me already, since I did attain standing, then walking. No one knew how, except my teachers and trainers, and the medical community did not accept much of what those teachers taught. You see, I did not really perceive myself at that time as a quad, but as a walking person. That was perhaps pivotal in my mindset. I was now wearing regular shoes, because I could. Other quads could not do so because of the possible pressure on their feet. I was developing arches, whereas before, I did not have them. My quadriceps were stronger, and I could sit and stand straight. No longer was I sinking into a curled up shrimp-like posture as some quads do. I was not falling into the wasted shape that most quads take. These were the very real behaviors and states I was attaining.

Dr. T.: You said that seeing yourself as a walking person was pivotal. What do you mean?

M. S.: I was no longer limited by the medical dogma of being a quad. I had been struggling to bust out of that mold. I had jumped a mental hurdle that would now permit me to think of the happy possibilities rather than only the morbid limitations prescribed by mainstream doctors. I may have just been fooling myself at the time, but it felt right. And, it turned out to be right!

Dr. T.: Do you think this limiting image is the problem for other handicapped people?

M. S.: Without any doubt. The physical damage is done within the neurological system, within the body, not typically the mind! Doctors, who are held in high esteem, tell the world that, based upon medical facts, a quadriplegic cannot regain much function, if any. They maintain this across the board. Physicians, psychologists, physical therapists tell us we cannot move! This is a powerful societal and consequent psychological imposition, and most have believed it.

Dr. T.: In your deepest understanding, to what do you attribute the fact that you made that mental leap, of believing you would regain function and walk? Was it one thing? Was it an accumulation of things over time?

M. S.: I think it was a combination of things. The ongoing positive input from so many great sources was cumulative, and eventually became manifest within my body through the agency of my mind. I thought deeply about these new and high ideas provided by the likes of Keith Magnuson, you, Dr. Trausch, Barbara Devine, and others, and actually believed them! From that act of believing, I attempted to act according to these ideas, and eventually they paid dividends. It was Dr. Dennis Waitely who wrote *The Psychology of Winning*, in which he said: "What the mind harbors, the body manifests." He may have been talking about disease: I believe one's negative thoughts generate disease. But, why can it not work in reverse: one's positive thoughts generate health? This principle was operative in me.

Dr. T.: If one believes this, what is it that stops any highly motivated person, from attaining everything he or she wants physically?

M. S.: I think it is because they don't believe it enough. They likely only buy into a small percentage of it, even though they talk the talk. If they really believed it wholeheartedly, it could happen. For example, as far back as 776 BC when the Greek people inaugurated the Olympic games, their Olympic ideal gave to the world an understanding that man reaches his greatest glory when body, intellect, and spirit are used simultaneously. Roger Bannister demonstrated this synergistic power when he broke what was until then the ceiling for running speed, beating the four-minute mile. He was only one and a half seconds under, but penetrated what was an enormous psychological barrier. Within a year, thirty-seven other runners came along and ran the mile under four minutes. Like that barrier, quads before me could not walk, should not walk, they were told. Now, people with crushed spinal cords all over the country are walking. The lion's share of this change is due to the shift in attitude regarding what a quad can do. Before me, the belief was that no chronic quad could walk. After me, many chronic quads walked. It changed the landscape of America in terms of the quadriplegic's possibilities.

Dr. T.: So, what is it then that stops a champion, a leader on this path, like you, from sustaining this level of belief?

M. S.: Perhaps it is the inability to continue on year after year, decade after decade, and eventually selling out to an easier way of life. Physical exhaustion. Coming to realize that the energy expenditure necessary to complete the task of walking without any help, and without any other, outside miracle, would be so great that the prospect of that expenditure looms larger than the goal of walking independently. That is the reason, along with deterioration of my hip joint due to a life-threatening staph infection some years ago, I cannot walk today as I did in the past.

Dr. T.: Based upon what you are telling me, what do you recommend other handicapped people do? Are there any shortcuts?

M. S.: Although this question would take another book to detail, in the big picture, they should aim for balance in their lives. Otherwise, the task is so great that they will begin to fragment.

Secondly, to carry this intense mental, physical, emotional and spiritual load, they must become a middle manager. You recall that middle managers were popular in the 1980's and 1990's, as liaison personnel, acting between the top executives and the mass workers. As unconventional as it may sound, handicapped people must become active managers of those workers who serve them. They must create an atmosphere of connectedness between all of their resources, their human capital, if you will, and be sure everyone gets credit for what they are doing. Whoever cleans you, moves you, and takes care of you, must receive recognition and appreciation. Maintaining such an atmosphere pays great dividends.

Third, they should try not to take themselves too seriously. They should just do the best they can with the resources they have. For example, one young man who was a helper of mine was from the Philippine Islands. He was one of thirteen provincial board members representing thirty-one Philippine cities. Although only twenty-seven years old, he was like a governor there, and administered whole provinces. He was well-spoken, and handled himself well. Ironically, he arrived in the United States and worked in a nursing home. All this, because he did not get reelected in his home country. I called him Sir Dino, even though he cleaned my toilet. I treated him with deep respect, even though he did my lowly chores. My perspective is that in the end we are all one, all the same.

"If you compare yourself to others, you may become vain and bitter, for always there will be greater and lesser persons than yourself.

—Desiderata

13

CELEBRITY

I had taken my first steps. I was a quadriplegic who walked! *"Physician, heal thyself"* are words that played in my head. Is this what that Bible passage meant? Had I healed myself? Had God healed me? Was I really healed? What did this mean? I was profoundly excited, yet somehow apprehensive. Why?

In Greek mythology, Aesculapius holds the distinguished honor of being the deity of healing. Although he was a mortal physician, he was so accomplished at curing people that he incurred the wrath of the gods. The god of the underworld, Hades, was so concerned that Aesculapius would undermine regular human infusions of the dark abode of the dead that he complained to the top god, Zeus, who downed Aesculapius with a thunderbolt. In the end, Aesculapius was brought to the heavens as a lesser god, and placed under stringent scrutiny by Mount Olympus.

Is there some unknown, mischievous, universal law that put me in this condition of a cripple to punish me? Was Einstein wrong in his belief that there is continuity, a benevolent order in the cosmos? That God does not play dice with His universe? Was I paying some ancient debt incurred in a former dimension? Could I really enjoy this fortuitous turn of events?

*   *   *   *   *   *   *   *   *   *

It was the early summer of 1982, and word traveled fast in the Chicago suburbs, and my life became frenetic almost overnight. Friends and relatives, and people who I did not even know were coming to visit me. Moms and dads with kids who were paraplegic, quadriplegic, traveled some distances, bringing their disabled children along with them. They wanted to see me, touch me, and ask me all manner of questions. Amazingly, it was not so much that they wanted to hear of my process, the sweat, the agony, the tears, how I came to do such an impossible thing. Rather, they just wanted to be in my presence and somehow take in the aura of one who had achieved something seemingly impossible. For me it was all very astounding. Although I was standing frequently, I had just begun to take steps, and still spent plenty of time in my wheelchair.

My brother had a friend named Mike Leonard, who was an NBC correspondent to the "Today Show". In July, Jim told Mr. Leonard about me, and the media wheels were set in motion. In the eyes of the world, what I had accomplished was nothing less than a miracle. So, in came dozens of newspaper reporters, writing about a walking quad. Since I am what is known as a C4–C5 chronic quad, having been crippled for over six years, it was miraculous. I had been confirmed as a lifelong quadriplegic, and relegated medically to this status forever. Here was a story!

139

The morning came when Mike Leonard and an NBC van pulled up to my house with a TV crew. People were everywhere, in the yard, on that lawn, and on the sidewalk where I had taken my first private steps weeks ago. It was a great day for me, in spite of the apprehension I was feeling about being on national TV. What do I wear? Even though it was hot summer, I wanted to wear long pants to cover the Foley catheter that ran down my leg to the urine bag. What do I say? Some of my nurses even showed up that day wearing makeup! Neighbors lined the sidewalk along Garland Place, the street on which I lived. I was so very pleased with myself. That day would last seven long hours.

The time came for Mike Leonard to interview me. He told me that he had played hockey for Providence College, and understood how important it was for an athlete who loved hockey to be able to play. He asked what it felt like, physically, to be paralyzed, especially immediately after the accident, lying there in the hospital. He asked about the things I had done to come to this point of walking, and what I intended to do with my life. I told him that I initially believed I would be able to "come back" and "get in the playoffs with my team." Our time together was delightful to me, for it represented tangible recognition of the fact that I had accomplished what no one else had. As the interview unfolded, I stayed calm and present to what was happening here on my home street. Having the TV cameras on me was a definite stressor, and my natural tendency was to be stiff. But, in the end, it went well.

Next came the part everyone had been waiting for: seeing me walk. Walking took a tremendous effort for me, an intense concentration and application of will. How happy I was, now that I had trained, and trained some more. Out on that yard in front of my house, as the cameras rolled, I got up from my wheelchair and walked across the lawn, pushing a lawnmower! Cheers rose from the crowd, and it was as if I was back on the hockey rink, performing with all the skill I ever had. I rose to the occasion and did not choke or freeze up. I was again the star. Now, it was my time, and my family's, to be recognized. The criticism we had taken from the mainstream medical community, and from skeptical acquaintances, was melting away in the appreciative applause. We were justified in everything we had done, and getting this acknowledgment for the time and effort we had put in was fabulous. In those few moments of pushing the mower, my life to that point since the accident, six long years ago, played out before me. Each and every time I had spoken about my goal of walking to anyone, I had been shot down in some way, criticized, made to look like I was delusional, a fool, a dreamer, not in touch with reality. These painful and saddening scars were deep within me. Yet, as I walked, freshly showered by the acclaim, those wounds softened and began to heal. I had manifested my dream.

After that day, Mike Leonard went to see the physician who had pronounced me a hopeless quadriplegic, Dr. Paul Meyer, to ask him, "How is it that a quad can walk?" Mike likely showed the tape of me walking with him to Dr. Meyer. Meyer told him that about half of spinal cord injuries regain some movement. I was furious. I felt this was a bullshit cover-up of the truth. He was protecting his own ass from discredit for having stated categorically that I would never walk. He even sidestepped the question of walking, through distraction, by talking about regaining "some movement." What do you do as a doctor when presented with videotaped proof that your medical pronouncement is false? This physician did not have any understanding of what was happening with me. No one really did. But I did. Barbara Devine did. Dr. Trausch did. Keith Magnuson did.

One month later, in August, we had a big breakfast party and watched the Today Show airing of my walkabout. Mom, Dad, and friends sat at various TV's and watched the four-minute clip taken out of the whole seven hours. Then it began. The phone calls started coming in. So many, in fact, that we had our phone number removed from the directory listing. Quads and families were calling from around the country. It was not long before a call came in from

USA Today. More phone calls. People were investigating how to get to me, and cleverly finding their way around the unpublished phone number. I found myself hiding from the onslaught. But, they just wanted to watch me walk. They wanted to know what I had done, both handicapped and able-bodied people. I told them what I had done, but only at a surface level. I didn't tell them about the blood, the effort, the energy expenditure, and the mind-bending application of will. I skimmed over the facts, hitting only the highlights, and then gave them what they wanted: to see me walk.

Except for a few exceptional souls that seemed to appreciate the grueling daily efforts I had put into the walking, visitors were not interested in how I got to this point. After some general descriptions of my current practices, I would perform for them. I did feel, however, that in spite of their surface interest in my journey, "quick fix" people were getting something at a deeper level, in spite of themselves. I came to realize that this something was hope. They all wanted hope. Here was a chronic quad, walking. "Maybe there is hope for me!" they thought.

This growing public interest caught the attention of investigative reporter, Bill Kurtis. At the time he was the CBS news anchor in Chicago. Mr. Kurtis contacted me and suggested narrating a film documentary on me at my home. It was for a portion of his TV program, called "Focus". He met me at home in Des Plaines, where he interviewed me in the kitchen. Then, I stood, held his hand, and we walked down the hallway with my helper in tow. He asked me a fascinating question. He said, "Do you think that you will be in physical therapy the rest of your life?" That question just about knocked me off my chair. I had never really thought about it. I genuinely thought that one day I would get better and not have to train any longer. And, as hard as I trained, I had to ask myself if I could keep up that intensity for the rest of my life? And, here is the disconcerting clincher: what if I couldn't?

Later Charles Kuralt from "The American Parade Show" would research me, and run a feature program of me walking on CBS national television. Because of these experiences, and the interest people were displaying in my having walked, I was becoming increasingly aware of the power of what I had accomplished, and its influence on even normal, healthy people. Of course, I cannot take all the credit. It was not just me who had achieved, but all those who had been at my side coaching, inspiring, supporting, and waiting on me.

As I hinted earlier, there was still a piece of unfinished business stewing in me. I had to go back and see Dr. Tom Fahey again! In spite of all my successes, his unthinking words, detracting from my goal to walk, had not healed. I arrived at his office sitting in my wheelchair. When he finally entered, I was waiting there with my helper. I slowly rose from my wheelchair and stood, facing him. Then, by myself, I walked across his office room, turned around and walked back to my wheelchair holding the hand of my helper. My leg braces? They had been sold to another quadriplegic at least a year earlier. Dr. Fahey stared at me for a moment. Then he turned, silently walked to his desk, sat down and put his feet up. I waited, facing him head on. He leisurely lit up a cigarette, turned to me and said, "Schwass, you sure faked the hell out of me!" What a physician! Dr. Fahey had made a shift, and in fact became interested in what I was doing, offering his help and expertise.

Quadriplegics, and other, able-bodied people, came to see me from the four directions, some to be evaluated by Barbara Devine on the Myoflex. She ran clinics, and at the end of each one, Barbara would ask me to get up and walk. We would have a crowd of quadriplegics and families watching, like a fashion runway, taking pictures to hurry home with to show to family members. "Pop! Pop! Pop!" went the cameras. It brought great joy to me. I had been accused of "chasing rainbows" by many, even within my close family members. I had watched indulgent expressions on the faces of so many who entered my life that had themselves completely accepted the "fact" that I would never get out of that wheelchair, never stand. What I had done was paying off in a grand fashion, and other deeply wounded youths could benefit. *Who is chasing rainbows now,* I thought.

One young quadriplegic who came to see me was Gary Horn. He lived in Manhattan and had what is called a C-5 injury that had left him paralyzed. There were obscure and intricate ways that networking had been creatively arranging getting him to me. Gary had a friend who lived in San Jose, California, who had read an article depicting my journey from confinement to a wheelchair to standing, in the September 22, 1982 issue of *USA Today*. The headliner had read:

WILL TO DISPROVE DOCTORS PUTS ATHLETE BACK ON FEET

USA Today, September 22, 1982

Having then read the article for himself, Horn, along with his chiropractor, made arrangements for them both to be flown to Des Plaines, Illinois to see me. They registered at a motel and immediately found their way to my door. Although in a wheelchair just like me, Gary was an imposing figure. He was a slim, six-feet-five inches tall young man, with long black hair, and an intensely inquisitive demeanor. His super-sized smile radiated his warmth and good nature. His face reflected intelligence and flowering insight. Dwarfing his wheelchair, he sat alongside his doctor and told me his story. In 1981, a near-fatal swimming accident broke his neck, leaving him in the hospital for eleven months. After that, quadriplegia.

Although his was a heartrending story, Gary was undaunted, and in fact one of the funniest guys I have met. His character depth, and spiritual interests matched mine, and would make us kin immediately, although I did not know it at the time of our first meeting. He and his chiropractor watched me walk. Their awe was obvious. Gary called me his hero, one who had "broken the mold for quadriplegics." He and his chiropractor asked many questions: "What is a typical day for you? What kind of therapy do you do? How long were you with Dr. Trausch and Barbara Devine? How long before you walked again after the accident? Who else did you work with? What do your trainers do? Who are they?" This went on for the entire weekend.

In these poignant questions, I could hear the quadriplegic's mantra: "How long am I going to have to be in this condition?" I answered Gary and his doctor in the best way I knew how. I told them who my trainers and guides were. I described to them how I had organized a complete discipline, including mind training, insight and inspiration, physical therapy, biofeedback, and a proactive, persevering attitude. In reflecting upon this encounter with Gary, and other paralyzed young men, women and children, I realize that I did not give myself much credit for the endless and intense hours of motivational work I had engaged in that led to my success. I had so recently been getting such an abundance of celebrity recognition from people, that I discounted the mental and psychological skills that I had acquired that would prepare me for the place at which I had arrived. The truth is, at the time I could not even comprehend what I had accomplished. I would only gradually come to that realization with the passage of years, and the slow but steady stream of wisdom that accumulated within me as a result of facing head-on my continuing ordeal.

In disclosing this, I am reminded of an event that occurred some years ago, in 1995 in Seattle, Washington, where the Special Olympics were being held. During the games, one event was conducted in which nine handicapped children were contestants. Standing at the starting line for the hundred-yard dash in the stadium, they readied themselves for the sound of the starting gun that would begin the race.

The pistol sounded, and so the special little company started out, tottering their way toward the finish line three hundred feet away. As the small assembly moved out, the crowd of parents, friends and supporters in the bleachers cheered them on. Then something happened. As the little troupe scrambled down the track, one small crippled boy stumbled and fell. He began to cry, and the other scampering children, upon hearing him, slowed and came to a stop. All turned around to see what had happened. The cheering in the bleachers stopped and a hush came over the crowd. To the surprise of everyone, the children began to walk back toward their fallen teammate.

Upon arriving there, they formed a disjointed circle around him. One little girl with Down's syndrome bent low and kissed him on the forehead, saying, "This will make it better." At that unpretentious, self-collected gesture, the hush that had blanketed the audience erupted into ten minutes of thunderous applause. It was the uncommon presence and unabashed benevolence of the little "athletes" that touched the hearts of everyone connected with those children. It was the shock of realizing what was *really* important that had impacted the core of each onlooker. Competition had transformed into compassion.

Likewise for me, it would be the magic of kindness, the enchantment of sacrifice, and the mutual toil and shared suffering with other beset brothers and sisters that would create a shift in how I perceived my world.

Meanwhile, the focus on me continued unabated, and almost without forewarning, it began to be routine. Dozens of articles were beginning to make their way into the news, but the spectacular effect of what I had accomplished was slowly wearing off on me. I was like a person on drugs, who after being on them a long time must necessarily habituate, and then need more of the same drug to get the old high. My drug was the enormous attention I had been getting, and the energy high it produced. Its effects were wearing off, and I needed a bigger fix. I needed to take it to another level. Now, I had to try to walk without having to hold someone's hand to balance me. To walk unassisted, by myself!

At the same time, something else was beginning to influence me. I was being driven as much now by social pressure to accomplish more, as by my original will to walk. That increasing pressure was stressing me in a way that rivaled the weight of being designated as a quadriplegic in the first place. Many people about me, my helpers, nurses, and family members, seemed also to be seeking the overflow of attention that was shed upon me. I had become the poster-boy for victory, the forerunner of an eventual Lance Armstrong, and those about me tended to soak up the nectar of recognition along with me. There seemed to be an emotional symbiotic relationship between us. I was a source of recognition for them; they were a source of survival for me. They needed me in different ways than I needed them, yet their needs were nonetheless valid.

But the growing attention from the public, and the excess responsibility I was taking on was making me mentally lethargic, and the sense of having to meet the needs of my helpers was draining. I was feeling an urge for more independence. *I need the next step!* Being able to walk alone, without any help, by getting even stronger and making deeper internal neural connections so as to move more naturally, would help me rely less on people in my life. *This would handle two birds with one stone,* I thought. By walking independently I would get more life-sustaining space away from both groups: those who needed to give me attention, and those who saw me as a source for filling needs for attention. This became my plan. This became my steady intention.

To continue the story, skip the Interview and go to the next Chapter.

Me as a baby, soaking up the rays

Already showing my athletic ability

Mom and me, my second Christmas

Grandpa O'Donnell and me on my first
Holy Communion Day

My favorite attire was always
a sports uniform

Beginning my Little League
baseball career

I'm in the center for soon to be stars
Larry De Salvo (left) and Ralph *"Roadrunner"* Dynek (right)

As good as it gets. . . raising my arms in victory after scoring a goal for my team

The four Co-captains of the 1976 IL State
High School Champs pictured with Coach
Meyer. From left to right, Don Hitzel,
Tony Salemi, Matt Berrafato, and myself;
Berrafato went on to become an
All-American high school goaltender

Me and my girl, Jill, the night of our Junior Prom. Little did I know this would be the only prom I would ever attend as a walking person

Me and Jill, shortly before the accident

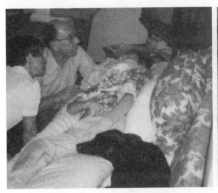

Man's best friend. . . Augie Dog gives me comfort shortly after my return from the hospital

My family was always around to give me support in those first long, dark days

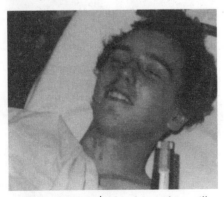

My first Christmas after the accident, still connected to the cervical tongs. I think the bottle of whiskey helped to put a smile on my face

The cervical tongs screwed me into one of man's worst nightmares: *the Stryker Frame*

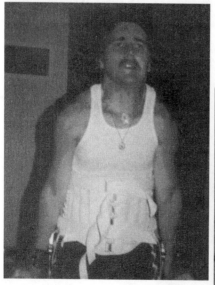

True grit. Determined to walk again

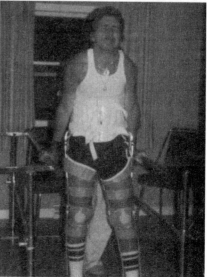

Almost there

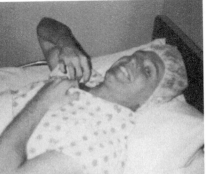

Wanna see my scar?

Achieving the impossible. Walking again
with a little help from my crew

My heroes. . . Keith Magnuson and
Stan Makita clowning around at a
fundraiser for my medical expenses

Keith Magnuson was there even when
I was still in leg braces

Me and Barbara Devine, one of the angels
sent to help me with my miracle

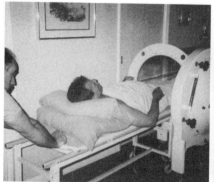

Man's great healer:
the Hyperbaric Chamber

Clear the roads,
I'm back behind the wheel

Facing the dragon. I'm standing over the
spot where my head crashed the end board
and rendered me quadriplegic

Giving a motivational talk to a group
of high school kids

Autographs please? I find that young kids
are uninhibited by my disability and ask
heartfelt questions

Mom and Dad and me, the day of my
graduation from DePaul University

Watch out!
Quad with a pole!

Inspirational speaking to businesses
and organizations

Dad had a rule: if you can walk, you can
work! The *NBC Today* show had
to film this trick!

Sharing writing notes in Southern
Wisconsin with Clarence at Twin
Cedars Retreat Center

A bittersweet moment: My team honors me by presenting me with the State Championship Trophy they won by beating the same team we were playing when I was injured. There are no coincidences in life!

In 2001, the Illinois State Hockey Association Championship's Game MVP was named after me. What a thrill!

Key members of the First Step Foundation: (rear left) my former teammates Bobby Miller, Matt Berrafato, Coach Gary Weber, Tony Salemi, Jill and Steve Duffy

INTERVIEW

Dr. T.: When you walked, who was it that was responsible for that? God? You? Or something else?

M. S.: I don't know. Without thinking too deeply about it, I would say it was a combination of those forces. Perhaps the whole thing was a divine plan to inspire other people, to make the world a little better place, and expand the small bubbles we live in. Perhaps an able-bodied person who has a mission in life might pull a little inspiration from me to help make the world a better place. Maybe we are all just players in a larger drama.

Dr. T.: Have you considered other justifications, other reasons for having the accident, and then achieving the ability to walk again?

M. S.: I have, but after long and careful examination, they do not make sense. I must make sense out of it all, and finding an acceptable meaning works. By far, most of the feedback I get from people I encounter is, "You have been an inspiration to me," or "You encourage me." It is the same thing even with children. It is why I have written this book and called it *Don't Blame The Game*, because it is one of the first things people ask me about: "Do you blame the person that checked you? Do you still like hockey?" These people are looking for meaningful ways to organize and think about and behave in regard to their own problems.

Dr. T.: What is the definition of healing to you?

M. S.: To somehow arrive at a place of peace within myself. Working on my body, mind, and spirit in order to obtain inner peace.

Dr. T.: When you went back to confront Dr. Fahey, did you get the personal satisfaction out of that encounter that you expected?

M. S.: More than that. I never expected any doctor to admit he was wrong at all. Further, I never thought he would do it in such a mild and kind way. He even wanted to get involved and help. He showed me what muscles to focus on and strengthen. In doing these things he gained my respect. I have been told, hundreds of times, that doctors who saw me walk handled their dismay by thinking it would have happened anyway. Or, that my injury was not really as bad as had been diagnosed. That is the kind of rationalization I got from most doctors, who were brainwashed by their own medical teachings, and afraid to stand out apart from, or beyond, their peers.

Dr. T.: This deeper understanding of the role medical people and places play in the world of disabilities is marvelous. How do you now look at the role of the Rehabilitation Institute of Chicago? Has your early, youthful blame remained?

M. S.: No. The growthful experiences I have had, and the disabled people I have met over the years, have shown me that the Rehabilitation Institute of Chicago was doing the best possible job it could do at that time, especially with the massive amounts of people coming through their doors. As a graduate of social work, especially, I now realize that they were all squeezed by insurance companies, limited coverage, and short staffing.

"This is the true joy of life. The being used for a purpose recognized by yourself as a mighty one. The being a force of nature rather than a feverish little clod of ailments and grievances complaining that the world will not devote itself to making you happy."

—George Bernard Shaw

14

VALIDATION:

INTO THE TERRITORY

The magic of my strong intention to show the world that it was possible for a quadriplegic to walk must have worked, because the opportunity came through Barbara Devine. Having been working with me, and a group of about a dozen quadriplegics on the Myoflex machine in Chicago, she announced that she was taking a position at the Sealy Hot Springs Spa in Cottonwood, Alabama, to treat patients coming to the spa. Her expertise with the Myoflex was getting recognition, and this mineral springs health clinic wanted her to set up shop there and demonstrate her success. She invited all of us to join her down there for several months as members of a therapeutic work group. She would exercise her physical therapy skills on us in an ideal atmosphere of therapeutic mineral waters. Of course, we all jumped at the opportunity. After a brief investigative visit in the fall of 1982, I took up residence at the Sealy, Alabama health resort January 7, 1983. I was just twenty-four years old, and had been living with my parents in Des Plaines. This was my first foray into the world of independence.

We would have to pay for this experience at Sealy Springs ourselves, but since Barbara Devine was so influential, she had arranged for the quadriplegics to get discounts on everything.

Sealy Hot Springs was noted for its steaming water, which comes out of the ground twenty-four hours a day, 365 days a year at a scalding 112 degrees Fahrenheit. It is then cooled down, by movement into various pools, to accommodate the sensitive human skin. This spring-fed water has never stopped, and is said to be loaded with a swarm of restorative minerals.

The idea behind mineral baths is that one will absorb some of the minerals through the skin while soaking in the soothing liquid. Health practitioners and doctors who ran the clinic believed that this absorption would benefit a body in a more natural way than would occur by the taking of a mineral supplement. I don't know if this is true, but the hot baths were good in themselves, simply because they felt good. The engulfing heat permeated my body to its core, exponentially increasing my sense of wellbeing.

The Spa staff also recommended that guests drink the water, which had been collected from two flowing six-inch pipes connected to the large pools where visitors were immersed. Once a week the staffers closed different pools, and workers scraped the sides to remove lingering minerals that had accumulated as a kind of reddish and off-white residue. Once cleaned, the pools were open to us again. We steeped in it, floated in it, and drank it from pitchers placed by the attendants. We inhaled its wafting steam. Our skin would turn orange from both the heat and the high mineral content. There could be perhaps no better heaven on the earth for a quadriplegic than being buoyed weightlessly upon these magical waters.

I was happy with the Sealy Hot Springs idea of lounging in their super water. Mother nature presents these wonderful nutrients through the earth, and people come from everywhere to seek this warm, moist, healing comfort. For me, being there with others who were also in physical trouble was helpful, not in the sense of misery loving company, but in the sense of having mutual support.

The Sealy Hot Springs staff presented to us other therapeutic opportunities, including chiropractic, electrical stimulation, IV therapy, massage, organic food prepared by a chef who was skilled in nutrient selection, and healthy ideas about body care. In addition, the spa provided chelation therapy, which entailed receiving circulatory cleansing agents through an IV.

My experience at the spa with Barbara Devine was just "divine," as always. Over and above our usual sweaty efforts with Barbara to make our bodies move, we patrons also had the daily opportunity to bask in the steaming elixir that characterized this paradise.

If all this were not enough, the people of Cottonwood, Alabama were a warm and friendly southern folk that made us feel wholly welcomed. The Spa's staff had heard of Barbara's work and demonstrated deference to her. I stayed at that spa for over six months, and it was one of the finest physical and sensual experiences I have ever had. In some significant way, the Sealy experience represented the medicinal images that played in my mind on the night of the accident, that all I needed was to get myself into a hot water bath.

* * * * * * * * *

It was in the spring of 1983, during my stay at the spa, and about nine months after I had taken my first steps for The Today

Show, that an unusual event occurred. One morning, two physicians appeared at Sealy Hot Springs to inquire about me. One was Dr. Wise Young, and the other Dr. Christian Ragnarsson. It seems that Mr. Robert Moody, of Moody National Bank and the American Insurance Company fame, had taken notice of my walking progress that had been exhibited in the media. It was not simply a perfunctory interest on Mr. Moody's part, for he was the father of an adolescent brain-injured child. His son, named Russell, had a brain stem injury, and could move his arms and legs, but had diminished cognitive abilities, and could not speak very well. Mr. Moody thought that Barbara Devine could work with Russell, and perhaps make a difference, based on the success she had had with me. Mr. Moody had explored the medical and psychological research for some treatment that would help his boy, but to no avail. He had hired both Drs. Young and Ragnarsson, who were researchers at New York University Bellvue Hospital, to investigate me: to determine whether I was a phenomenon or a fake! They had come to determine if my recent walking experience was just some hoax that had been conjured by an opportunistic mind. Being vigilant scientists, they conjectured that a confederate of mine was secretly moving my legs, or that some strong electrical intervention was being enlisted to simulate movement, and that through these secret devices I had deceived the media.

I was highly intimidated by their appearance, and in spite of their suspicions, I wanted to look good and to put on a good show. We all did, even though they had come specifically to scrutinize me. So, I went through my training and walking exercises. These researchers, whom I expected to be critical, judgmental, demeaning, even suspicious, turned out to be friendly, kind, and genuinely interested in all of us. They viewed and analyzed our workout sessions and seemed to genuinely enjoy themselves. Even though a couple of other quadriplegics were making progress, no one was able to really walk besides me, and because of this they affectionately called me "The Champ." Everyone wanted to get where I was, and I quickly became the focus of the doctors from New York. For their part, they were appropriately impressed, and said so. Dr. Wise Young reported that there was no doubt that *"Michael Schwass was using his own legs for ambulatory movement."*

Several important things resulted from this encounter in Cottonwood, Alabama. Doctors Young and Ragnarsson became believers, and advocates of my endeavors to walk, and of the unconventional notions and interventions I had enlisted. They were doing research for spinal cord injuries at New York University, and returned there to spread the word of what I had achieved. They showed films of me walking, and informed the National Institute of Health, in Bethesda, MD., and other interested investigators, what they had witnessed. Because of the documented evidence of my own walking, and the gains of the other spinal cord injured residents at Sealy Spa, new research to study such injuries was funded at the National Institute of Health. This research eventually resulted in the creation of a drug called methylprednisolone. Today, that very medicine, when injected within eight hours of a spinal cord injury, can stop paralysis.

Years later, it would happen that on November 29, 1992, Dennis Byrd, defensive end with the New York Jets, would break his neck during a game in a freak collision with a member of his own team. Knocked to the ground, he lay there without moving, paralyzed. By then physicians knew about methylprednisolone. As a result, Dennis was quickly taken to the hospital and injected with the drug, and eventually escaped paralysis! This incident would mark the beginning of new hope for spinal cord injury victims—and it would indirectly be because of the seminal work I had done to walk.

Dennis Byrd is likely not a quadriplegic because of my earlier contributions, and the work of those who watched me attain my goal. It may be that Dennis Byrd owes his life to the grueling commitment to excellence that we engaged in. In my thinking, the implications of these events cannot be overstated.

Ironically, and sadly, many times people who come into my life, even friends, have said to me, "Mike, have you heard about this new drug that stops paralysis if injected within a few hours of a spinal cord injury? If only they would have given you that shot when you had your accident." When people say something like this to me, I hear words play out for me in my head, *Little do they know that it is because of my motivation, my work, that this injection was even developed in the first place.*

*   *   *   *   *   *   *   *   *   *

Not long after the doctors from New York University left Sealy Spa, a day came for me that was the most exciting public experience of my young life. It was March of 1983, and I was just twenty-four years old. Due to the glowing reports provided by Drs. Young and Ragnarsson, I was invited by the renowned Robert Moody, who had been the catalyst who brought Drs. Ragnarsson and Young together, to speak at a convention center in Texas before an international gathering of neurosurgeons and other prominent guests.

Mr. Moody flew Barbara and me, with my helper and Barbara's son in tow, first class from Sealy Springs to Galveston, Texas. We then took a limo to the Galveston Oceanside Marriott, where we were escorted to the top floor restaurant, wined and dined, and treated like celebrities. After eating like kings and queens at an all-expense paid feast, we then used the pool and spa, and visited the shops before being escorted to the Gulf of Mexico to drink in the peaceful evening ocean. What a gargantuan treat!

In the morning, I worked out with my trainer, was showered, dressed, and readied for lunch, were I would meet Mr. Moody for the first time. My initial impression of Mr. Moody was that I had expected him to be taller than he was. He was well dressed, and had a neatly combed head of black, thinning hair. He was quite reserved, yet emitted a controlled aggressiveness. He carried himself in a purposeful way, and seemed to be aware of absolutely everything. It was as if something was driving him at every instant, and each movement he made seemed deliberate.

Mr. Moody never said very much to us, but we felt fully enveloped in his commanding aura. I felt an instant respect for this man. His status fairly demanded it. He seemed never satisfied with sitting and enjoying himself in the moment, but was brimming with energy, and gave the impression that he had much on his mind. Perhaps these qualities are what had made him such a successful businessman.

Mr. Moody informed Barbara and me that we were the main attraction for the conference, which would be attended by fifty very prominent neurosurgeons from around the globe, as well as other medical and notable persons. I was there to demonstrate that a quadriplegic could actually walk. I was to be the one to provide living proof to Mr. Moody's collection of scientists. His more personal motivation, I assumed, was to use me to generate interest in further research on spinal cord and other related injuries, from which his son would eventually benefit.

On the day of the conference, the convention center was filled with expectation, along with predictable skepticism. The time came for me to be introduced, and I was ready. I got up out of my wheelchair and walked across the entire stage, with helpers on either side of me for balance. I applied my will, and walked the walk. I was elated. However, I should have known what the reaction of medical people would be.

The surgeons did not believe what they were seeing as it unfolded before their eyes. Some silently left their seats, ascended the stage, and lifted my pants to see if I was wired to a robot or computer. They suspected I was being externally animated, and was simulating walking through the agency of a machine! But, how could they have known, let alone understand, that through the inspiration of Keith Magnuson, the motivational and mind training of Dr. Clarence Trausch, the skills and perseverance of Barbara Devine, plus my willpower and determination, I had created alternative bio-pathways for my brain circuitry to send messages to my leg muscles.

The map is not the territory. One who knows only the map does not know the territory. I had learned the map. I had also trekked the territory. With this public event, I believed that I had now accomplished something significant in the world, in spite of doctors' suspicions. I had won. I was, in a way, the surgeon's equal, or even their superior for a moment; not their prey, as I had been for far too long.

I reveled in the fact that research representatives from Baylor and other prominent universities were present to witness the event. I was happy that Texas Governor John Connelly was there, too, the man who some twenty years earlier had been injured by a killer's bullet during the assassination of President Kennedy in Dallas. Horrifying memories shot through my mind when I noticed that he was wearing noticeable bandages about his neck and shoulder, the result of recent surgery to further repair the original damage.

I watched the neurosurgeons, especially, as they cut into their steaks that day. I could not help but imagine that these were the same motions they would make as they cut into the fleshy nervous systems and bony spinal columns of a human body. I had so frequently been one of those pieces of meat on their cutting table. I had far too often been the helpless carcass under their knives.

I came away with a great sense of satisfaction in having changed my relationship with those in the medical establishment. What I had done that day in Galveston counted, and could not be refuted by a constricted and obsolete theory based on the limitations of the body. I had not just walked before them. I had sailed.

To continue the story, skip the Interview and go to the next Chapter.

MEDICAL EVALUATION

The following is an excerpt from a March 1983 letter written by Dr. Wise Young, Ph.D., M.D., then Associate Professor of Neurosurgery and Physiology at New York University, to Robert Moody. Mr. Moody had engaged Dr. Young to determine whether or not Michael Schwass had really achieved the ability to walk without aid of some secret or computerized device, since it was known to be impossible for a chronic quadriplegic to walk.

Dear Mr. Moody,

You have met Mike Schwass in Texas. A C4-5 quadriplegic, he had some sensory preservation shortly after injury, which according to current medical dogma should confer a more favorable prognosis. But Mike had no motor function at all in his legs for several years, and required a body brace to sit in his chair. As you saw, he is now able to stand independently for long periods of time, to walk distances of 50 feet or longer, to manipulate his torso to turn. Over the four months between the time I first saw him in November and now, he has improved. His stride is longer and stronger. His stamina has increased. He can stand and balance for relatively long periods of time on just one leg. There is no question that he will eventually be able to use his legs for routine walking. I credit the functional return to his tremendous motivation to walk, the intense walking program, and the astute physical therapy.... .

Sincerely,

Wise Young, Ph.D., M.D.
Associate Professor of
Neurosurgery and Physiology

INTERVIEW

Dr. T.: Mr. Moody was apparently a very highly motivated man with a purpose. Can you compare yourself to Mr. Robert Moody? How were the two of you similar? Different?

M. S.: We both had single-mindedness of purpose and high motivation, steadfastness, and willingness to do whatever it took to accomplish any goal. However, Mr. Moody was from an entirely different socioeconomic status. He had the ability to move people using his social and financial status to get what he wanted. Although I have certainly been guilty of some manipulation in my life, it is not my nature to move people using whatever status I have acquired.

Dr. T.: Do you believe that whatever power is operating in you that promoted your ongoing gains, belongs to Mr. Moody and others as well?

M. S.: Although I was never very close to him, I think I appreciated, and perhaps acquired a part of that nature or personality just by knowing that such intense and focused people may also have a sensitive side to them. Mr. Moody was penetrating into the unknown by having me come down there to Galveston. I was just beginning my inspirational and motivational career work, so I saw our similarities and enjoyed them. My status was just beginning to grow, and so I marveled at his already-existing status. What stands out most is the risk he took in finding a solution for his son, by financing a program that was wholly controversial. He stuck himself out in front of his peers, put his reputation on the line, and publicly supported this unconventional program based upon a belief that it was possible for quadriplegics to walk.

Dr. T.: Today, what is your impression of the experiences you had with the surgeons gathered by Mr. Moody? Is it relevant for you?

M. S.: It is irrelevant now, because now I don't care what they think. But then, I was invested in pleasing them because I so much wanted to walk, and therefore I got involved in their value systems. Now it is accepted all over the country that some quads walk. I look back and ask myself why was I so concerned about winning them over? Perhaps it was my ego needing recognition. It could have been my wanting to discredit the medical doctrine about quadriplegia, and to expose its shallow, contracted thinking. Or, to damage the surgeons' status and power, to punish them because they had mistreated me so much in the past. Or, further, to attack anything that threatened my hope of walking. Probably, it was a combination of all those things.

"I have not failed. I have just found 10,000 ways that won't work."

—Thomas Edison

15

A NEW RELATIONSHIP

After the weekend in Galveston, we flew back to Sealy Spa. Upon returning there, I resumed my experiences in the springs and the work with Barbara. However, circumstances were about to change. As a result of our demonstration for the neurosurgeons in Texas, Barbara had been solicited by Robert Moody to work for him. He offered her six thousand dollars a month to move the entire Sealy group of quads, including me, to Galveston to continue therapy with spinal cord injuries.

Mr. Moody's offer was serendipitous, for it prompted my fuller recognition that something had shifted within me, as well. I realized that I had become complacent and was not working as hard and diligently as I knew I must. I had tried every conceivable method with Barbara of walking independently—in the water, on land, kneeling, strapped to machines that improved blood flow by tipping me upside down—but had failed! I simply could not get my balance, but always had to hold onto something. A change was in the wind for me. I just had to get away from helpers, as I knew them. To do so, however, I would have to take on an even more weighty and pervasive responsibility.

*　*　*　*　*　*　*　*　*　*

After some deliberation, Barbara accepted the research position in Galveston, and in June of 1983 moved there with her assembly of quads, without me. Rather, I decided to visit Florida and work with a new physical therapist I had discovered named Ray Cralle'. Before actually relocating to Florida, however, I journeyed back home to Des Plaines for what I planned would be a short visit.

A whole year passed while I did my daily therapy at home, took nutrition classes, and did some light public speaking on motivation and spinal cord injury awareness to service clubs, religious organizations, and various other groups.

As fate would have it, during this period, I delivered a lecture on the psychological effects of spinal cord injuries for the Northern Illinois University nursing program in De Kalb, Illinois, and met a student nurse named Maria Harmon. Shortly after the lecture, she contacted me to tell me she was looking for a summer job. However, I did not hire her because a chiropractic physician had recommended another, more experienced nurse. Typically, student nurses were a part of my summer program because my other nurses needed to take care of their school age children, dismissed from their classes for the summer.

As time passed, however, Maria sought me out more and began to ask me to join her for the movies, for dinners, and for concerts. I agreed, and the frequent contact brought us gradually closer. Since I had not had a girlfriend in so long, having this woman close to me was quite unusual, and appealing. I was twenty-five years old now, and had never had sexual contact as a quad. I didn't really know how to behave with a female any longer.

Was I attractive? Could I present myself properly on dates? No longer be confined in my chair watching tedious TV, alone? Was I capable of having sex? Did my sexual organs even work? My body looked fairly good, especially since I put it through such grueling training every single day. So, I thought, *I'll give it a try and see what it's like.* Because of Maria's experience in nursing, I didn't need to have a helper or nurse on our dates. She would automatically know how to help me given any eventuality. Otherwise, she could be easily coached through something unfamiliar to her—but commonplace to me!

And so it happened. And the sex was fascinating! Who better than a student nurse to learn these things from? As time passed we became even closer. I was experimenting in the world of women. Could this really be happening to me? As a quad, I had long ago surrendered any hope of having a relationship in favor of the necessities it took to get through each hour of a day. I was still living at my parents' home in Des Plaines. So, to be alone, Maria and I would sometimes go to secluded places to enjoy each other.

Another year passed, me doing my workouts and public speaking, Maria attending Nursing School. In the spring of 1985, she graduated from Northern Illinois University with a degree in nursing. We promptly moved together to Del Ray Beach, Florida, and lived in an apartment. This way, Maria and I were both together, and I was closer to Ray Cralle', whom I intended to continue to work with.

These were not the only reasons for moving to Florida. I also chose it for its distance from Illinois. It represented getting away from people who knew me, specifically, my family. Their good Catholic religious attitudes were so conservative that I would have had to justify to them why I was moving in with a girl. Not wanting to go through this pious gauntlet, Florida represented an escape route. Looking back upon it however, this reaction was only my personal fears about what society might think about the famous Mike Schwass living in sin!

After a year with Maria in Florida, now 1986, our relationship began to break down. She became disenchanted with my paralysis, or my insecurities about myself, or both. Additionally, Maria needed so much attention that I did not have the energy to minister to her emotional needs and to get my own physical needs met as well. And, during our year of living together, she had grabbed onto me, and fallen in love with a rock. Her own poor family life, which lacked emotional support, had led her to me. I had become aware of this during our first year together in Illinois, but our relationship had been an opportunity for adventure—and I was an adventure-seeker. I got hurt a lot. Maria got hurt. We broke up. It was the first time I had been actually living on my own since the accident.

During our year together in Florida, I was seeing Ray Cralle', an expert physical therapist who worked in retraining children with neuro-physical disorders. Ray was a highly intellectual and well-versed professional who reminded me of Barbara Devine in the way he approached his treatment modalities. Physically, he was huge, an ex-basketball player from Virginia, and an imposing figure standing about six-feet-six.

His practice was like an art, and he performed physical therapy in ways I had never heard about, or read about, in any research material. His method was to use a combination of ice and high-tone vibrations to stimulate muscle action. He would rub ice on a muscle site, and simultaneously apply electrical vibrations—what he called neuromuscular facilitation—to get stiff, inefficient, hyper-toned muscles to relax.

I worked with him for months while living with Maria, until he became overloaded. His interventions were unique, and many others were seeking his treatment. Since his was a one-man show, his work eventually became diluted as a result of spreading himself too thin. Progressively, I spent longer and longer hours waiting on his therapy table looking up at the ceiling. In my growing impatience, I would frequently think: *Here I am spending my precious time waiting for Ray Cralle'. What kind of life is this?*

Although his program was to some extent working for me, I didn't want to stay any longer. I was only seeing slight improvement in my walking, and even less in my overall mobility and balance. I was impatient. The changes during most of that year were not dramatic enough for my high-strung nature. The cost of waiting longer to see more improvement outweighed any gains I was making under his direction.

Occasionally, as I lay there on his table, I was beginning to have fantasies about being back on the Stryker bed. This was the clincher. I had to leave. I would find another, even more dramatic method to make progress. These collective circumstances and thoughts brought both my relationship with Maria, and with Ray Cralle' to an end. I moved back to Chicago. Alone.

Once back in Chicago, in the fall of 1986, I reconnected with Barbara Devine, who had completed her contract with Robert Moody and was again working in the Midwest. After examining me, she told me that my neck was very weak, and that it had never been aligned correctly. She recommended that I meet with and have a neck evaluation by Dr. Carl Kao, a noted Washington D.C.-based neurosurgeon. This represented what I consider a fortuitous next step in my search for more healing input.

I met Dr. Kao in Las Vegas at a therapy clinic where he was evaluating other spinal cord injury patients for their surgery potential. From a distance, Dr. Kao was a stocky and unimpressive figure: five-feet-five inches tall. To meet him up close, however, was another matter. He was a frightening looking man, and until then, was the most intense man I have ever met—more intense even than Robert Moody. His face showed signs of wear, worry, concern, and brilliance all at the same time. He was also painfully meticulous, and wore an impeccable three-piece suit over his smooth, olive colored skin. Much to my relief, however, his manner was not like his appearance. He turned out to be a kind man, and so very skillful. When he reached for a pencil and drew a replica of my x-ray film on paper, I could not tell the difference between the drawing and the x-ray.

Dr. Kao's evaluation disclosed that the fifth vertebra in my spinal column was pressed backwards, and imposing itself into the spinal canal. He told me that the original surgeons had not aligned it properly, or the weight of walking had begun to compress it. The X-rays Dr. Kao presented to me clearly showed, even to a layman's eyes, the vertebral bone pressing against the spinal canal. This was responsible, he said, for the fact that I had begun to choke on food. In the months prior to Dr. Kao's evaluation, I had needed to keep a glass of water nearby to help wash down stuck food. Obviously, my neck had not been repaired to accommodate a walking quadriplegic!

In addition, it seemed that all the standing and steps I was taking in my walking efforts were moving and compromising the C-5 vertebral body, which was right at the center of the original crushed spinal vertebrae.

Another flaw he discovered was, during my original surgery in 1975, the neurosurgeon had introduced an acrylic material in the vertebral body. This material had been chosen by him to fill the hole in my neck that had resulted from the explosion of tissue ignited by my airborne encounter with the hockey rink end-boards. That substance was now jamming the spinal canal and impinging on what nerves remained in my damaged neck.

Dr. Kao explained that he would remove the acrylic substance and use bone from my hip, along with a metal plate, to fuse the damaged joint together. And on April 2, 1987, this little Taiwanese-born surgeon walked into the operating room and performed surgery on my neck standing on a stool.

As I recovered from the six hours and forty minutes of surgery that day, I came to understand that as a result of the operation my arms were re-paralyzed. This side effect, due to additional nerve damage sustained during the extensive cutting, left me with no alternative but to go through intense physical therapy to get them to move. I was outraged! I was sad. I felt despair that I would never be able to regain my arm movement. At some level however, I now admit, I was enjoying the rest. I had made so much progress in arm and hand movement that I had come to be able to do many things for myself, including grooming and eating. Now, people again had to feed me, and brush my teeth, and I was confined to a hard, two-piece Philadelphia Collar that would be wrapped around and strapped to my neck for three months, while living in Des Plaines.

The collar was a framework contraption designed to protect the neck. It had an egg-holder arrangement in front to support my chin. In the back, a brace kept my neck and chin in perfect alignment so that the bone surgically taken from my hip and placed into my neck would have a chance to fuse. This hipbone material had been put in my neck to replace the original acrylic material that was deteriorating. Into this jumble went a final complement of six metal screws. To this day, I still have screws in my cervical spine. I am the bionic man! This concoction, this bio-metal patchwork, has so far prevented my neck from re-breaking.

This whole potential breakdown of my neck, suspected by Barbara Devine, presented yet another predicament, and a delay in my program to walk independently. Being ever-so-familiar with having surgery on my body, I knew that this new neck operation would require a long recovery process, as it did. I had been on a whirlwind path, working out, speaking, studying, walking, having a relationship, and it was showing by the toll it had taken on my poor body. It seemed the moment was right for a break, so to speak. Time to think. Having this surgery was a blow to my program, not to mention my body. But, it was also to be a kind of "tranquility medicine" for my nonstop obsession with keeping on the move.

Another enormous problem prior to Dr. Kao's operation was around money. Although I had been working, I never made enough capital to finance the kind of costs associated with major surgery. The major medical health insurance that had originally covered my accident was exhausted, and no company would ever cover me again.

Enter Keith Magnuson again! Ten years after the first roast, he offered to organize another fundraiser. This was a roast of just Keith Magnuson and Stan Mikita, organized by Linda Johnson, Jerry

Watson, and Dick Cronin, who were friends of my family. They were instrumental in raising enough funds for me to have the operation.

To continue the story, skip the Interview and go to the next Chapter.

INTERVIEW

Dr. T.: Were women attracted to you? How so?

M. S.: More women were attracted to me than I knew of, or gave credit to. My feelings of inadequacy around my injury kept me from perceiving frequent attraction to me. I knew what they did not know about a spinal cord injury: how involved and time consuming it was. All they saw was a kind of handsome guy showing up at an athletic event, or a movie. I, however, projected my own reaction onto them, and dismissed their interest in me. Before attending a public event, most of my day was built around getting ready. It was a whole ordeal no one was privy to. Women only saw the end product, and sometimes it looks nice.

Dr. T.: What were the women with whom you got involved looking for?

M. S.: I think they were attracted to my inner strength, my discipline, and my prestige. I was a role model, and they took what they needed. These motivations did not come clear to me until I started walking, in 1982. I was gaining more inner peace by then and could more easily see into their motives. Before that, my own poor self-image prevented me from being tuned to the intentions and personal motives of people who were necessarily close to me.

Dr. T.: Did your relationship with Maria contribute anything to your life's journey?

M. S.: Absolutely. I loved Maria. When she lost interest in me, it damaged my identification with my stardom. That hit to my ego made me realize I could no longer only invest myself in enhancing my physical prowess. I opened my mind to finding a higher value in life, and to turning my attention toward it. I might even say that, by default, she put me more directly on a spiritual path.
Our separation awakened me to the truth that physical achievements, walking and stardom, would not carry me through life's vagaries emotionally, psychologically, or spiritually. She was the one who helped me move from a personal level of functioning to a transpersonal level, from the physical to the metaphysical. The pain I experienced after our breakup was the catalyst. Having someone like Maria no longer attracted to me generated disillusionment with my material pursuits. I became disappointed with the physical, and turned my head toward the spiritual.

Dr. T.: Are you still as high-strung and impatient as you were, say when you were forty?

M. S.: No. I learned that life has many dead ends, and that kind of intensity is damaging. I endeavor to survive rather than to look for glory, to accept what is rather than to think that there is some kind of pot of gold at the end of the proverbial rainbow. Much of my impatience was fueled by underlying delusions of grandeur, and seeking to have a wonderful life, a kind of heaven on earth.

Dr. T.: As you reflect on it, did you do the right thing by not continuing physical therapy with Ray Cralle'? Were you too impatient?

M. S.: I still believe it was the right thing to discontinue my work with him. I was beginning to build my own psychic identity, to which he had contributed. In addition, I saw that improvements I had been making early on in his treatments were tapering off and reaching a plateau. Putting those two things together made the move easy.

Dr. T.: Tell me about your operations, overall. Did you have too many? Not enough? Did they work? Were you looking for the wrong thing in having them?

M. S.: Not every major surgery I endured was elective, although all were calculated risks right from the start, with each offering some hope for the future. The first three surgeries, at Lutheran General Hospital and at John Wesley Hospital, contributed to needing the fourth, which was done by Dr. Kao. The fifth was experimental. The sixth was just to correct the fifth, and to keep me from dying. But, sometimes I would begin to lose touch with just where I was at, or I'd begin to deteriorate. Then I would get it in my head that I just had to do something to improve my worsening condition and would run the idea of a surgical intervention by family, friends, and mentors, seeking a solution. The feedback they gave me helped, but I'd ultimately make a decision. Of course, I tried everything else first—alternative medicine, physical therapy, even radical interventions—to avoid surgery.

"The most beautiful thing we can experience is the mystical. It is the source of all true art and science."

—**Albert Einstein**

16

SPIRITUAL TRANSFORMATION

Dr. Kao's surgery, and the resulting weakness and loss of ground had worked on me. I was no longer bulletproof. The body that I so restlessly prompted and prodded could fail me, not only from the outside, but also from within. That core essence of willpower and self-confidence that was so hard-won with Dr. Trausch, could fade, left unnourished. I began to realize just how fragile my body and mind were, and the consequent uncertainty of my whole journey to walk independently.

I had to start again, and relearn so many things, like moving my arms by means of pulleys and cords, trying frantically to propel myself in a wheelchair, struggling to brush my teeth, shave my face, and feed myself. I did just that, spending energy as it came to me, re-encountering and wrestling with old challenges presented anew. I exercised as much as the accumulating energy permitted. When there was extra, I enlisted it to push into a full upright stand.

Lurking in the background of all this primal effort following the surgery, and perhaps prompted by it, was a deeper, psychic concern. My basic question about having had this operation was a philosophical one. To be or not to be: would it have been better to endure the encroaching debility and eventual crumbling of my physical body; or better to have the operation and then necessarily retrace years of work just to arrive at where I had been before the operation? Reflecting back upon the whole issue, a light dawned. It seemed academic, really. The question that so troubled me was moot: either way, I would have surrendered a great deal of ground.

During the forced time alone with myself, while convalescing, some in Dayton, Washington where the operation had taken place, some in my parents' home, in Des Plaines, something happened to me. The desperate fight I put up to regain strength and mobility did affect, did alter, my sense of identity. I had for the first time genuinely hit the bottom of the barrel. In the last five years, being a superstar, I had forgotten what it was like to be a true quadriplegic. I had been down so often before, but I had never plumbed the depths of my desolation. Bedridden and alone, having lost Maria, having to so laboriously relearn the many hard-won skills that I had come to take for granted, an impending shift was germinating in my consciousness, of what life for me was to be about.

I ploddingly came to realize that the purpose of life was bigger than the small goal I had assigned to it. I must make a shift from being the celebrity puppet, to being a man with a life of soul-nourishing purpose. Through this most recent trial, the operation and long convalescence, I was being seasoned for a shift within my all-important goal of walking independently. I needed a more enlightened perspective.

Through a process of long and deep transforming meditations during my convalescence, I came to see that my vision had been too small, too narrow, too self-serving. I needed more compelling meaning from my existence than just an unyielding drive to walk independently. In these deep reflections, I came to see that I wanted to go back to college. To have a real girlfriend. To speak to the world about my trials. To contribute something to humanity, and to add to making it better! I was getting poised for something more vital. In my fervor, I wanted to create heaven on earth.

In August, 1987, about four months after the surgery, having recovered enough to get up and onto my feet, I actually started walking again. Hallelujah! In concert with the insights I had so recently gained about meaning, the first thing I did was to research the requirements for membership in the distinguished National Speakers Association (NSA). I also began thinking about what arrangements would be necessary for me to return to school and get a college degree. And, while about this business, as destiny would have it, I met Audrey.

To continue the story, skip the Interview and go to the next Chapter.

INTERVIEW

Dr. T.: What was the essence of your transformation?

M. S.: Does one keep up what one has striven for so long? Give up hope when reaching what appears to be a dead end? Everything that I had gained at lower levels—walking independently, intimate relations, material gains, recognition—seemed to be a dead end.

Dr. T.: How did that dawn on you?

M. S.: Just by being silent. Just by being alone with myself, long weeks in bed, lying there deep in reflection. I think it was Wayne Dyer who said: It is the silence between the notes that makes the music. The music for me was "Who am I? Where am I going? What am I going to do? Why do it?"

Earlier, as I tripped off to Florida with Maria, my thinking was that life must be more glitz and glory, and that everything would be smooth. I was deeply involved in and focusing on the relationship, and had to some extent set aside my psychospiritual pursuits. Some of your earlier teachings, that I had disregarded, even tried to disprove, were not going away. You had warned me that unexpected events would arise to test me, and I did not like that. You said, for example, that being in close quarters with another person would bring up unfinished business—old emotional injuries—that would need to be faced. I resisted that, flew off to paradise, and voilá, the whole thing became a big pot of psycho-stew, a recipe for disaster. After breaking up with Maria, I returned to you for a refresher course, for guidance and discipline, to see how these truths fit into the scheme of my life. I was searching for answers to the meaning of life. I had the opportunity to bring those waiting principles into focus during my obligatory convalescence after the surgery.

Dr. T.: Is your life of integrity a necessity to maintain that "soul-nourishing" purpose?

M. S.: Mandatory. I am forced to be a better person as a quad than I would have been as a healthy man. However, I'd like to be able to at least experiment with more adventures.

Dr. T.: Do you believe, in spite of sticking like glue to your high principles, that some lessons will be learned through experiences that compromise those principles?

M. S.: I think that any adventures I would want to go on would not violate any of my principles, because the activities I think of are just so common that everyone does them. Like climbing a mountain, water skiing, parasailing. As a quad, to experience them would be a thrill.

"Love one another, but make not a bond of love. Let it rather be a moving sea between the shores of your souls."

—**Kahlil Gibran, The Prophet**

17

THEN CAME AUDREY

Audrey Jans was a physical therapist living in Hoffman Estates, Illinois, and working at Humana Hospital. We had met through a mutual acquaintance, another physical therapist in Chicago. Audrey happened to be the only therapist in the Midwest who employed a unique apparatus, an underwater walking device, in her practice. It consisted of a treadmill that was placed in a pool, so that a body could be suspended in water while attempting to walk, weightless, on the treadmill portion. What a simple and yet amazing idea! I could practice walking without any body weight — like being on the moon, or in the weightlessness of space.

Audrey's device, and her exercise program, were good for me in the beginning. But, with time I realized that being weightless was cumbersome and that I was exerting too much effort trying to negotiate the weightlessness rather than truly walk. Also, in the cold

Midwest winters, I could hardly endure going out into the freezing cold after a hot water workout. In addition, there seemed to be no long-term gains from it. The device worked well as a jump-start on walking, but little more, at least for me. So, I decided to stop it around Thanksgiving in 1987.

While this technical and professional portion of my work with Audrey was ending, a relationship was developing between us. It happened really very quickly. I liked her, but didn't have any designs on her. She apparently enjoyed my company, as well.

On one occasion before I ended my water-walking sessions with her, I happened to be in Humana Hospital with my helper. It was at a time when Audrey would not have been there. We were surprised to see each other in this non-professional situation, and visited. She invited me, and my helper, to join her and some other friends for drinks, since she was ending work shortly. I agreed, and we all ended up at a local restaurant and bar called Mrs. P and Me.

Once there, my helper tugged me in my wheelchair up some twenty-one steps to an intimate loft where Audrey and her friends were ensconced. It seemed to me that every last person in the place watched my helper navigate me up each one of those stairs. It didn't bother me, however, since I was well dressed and feeling good. So confident had I become with my newly developing internal image that my thinking went: *Who wouldn't want to date me or be seen with me? After all, I have gone through that April operation with Dr. Kao. It was devastating. It was traumatic. He warned me that I could die on the operating table. I have looked death in the eye. I have survived, and I am recovering lost ground. I have overcome!*

The underlying drive for my exuberant attitude was this: I was carrying the idea and the experience of having faced my own death. In addition, memories of how much I had endured and overcome during the past decade were germinating a new and supremely confident outlook within me. I was above and beyond all of the petty opinions and judgments of everyone! My pre-existing adequate character strength had, through the gauntlet of the most recent surgery and its setbacks, mutated into a deep and superlative self-confidence.

From that point on, there was a shift in the way I thought about life. Although I was still pursuing the goal of walking independently, I was not in bed with it, so to speak. I was no longer addicted to it. Out of that surgery's trauma came the realization that there was more to life than just walking independently. Coupled with the intimacy and acceptance I was receiving, I realized more than ever that living each day as best I could, and with love for people, was more important than anything else I had ever done. To a certain extent, this expanded perspective was making me qualitatively a better person. I was a work in process.

It was this "new me" that was in place when I went to the bar to meet Audrey and her friends. This was my first social contact with her, but it included her friends as well. It was okay with me because it was one of my first social sorties since Maria. The evening went just fine, and my helper, Tom, and I dropped Audrey off at her home at four in the morning.

What followed was a series of phone calls between us, in which Audrey would just talk about her parents, job, relationships, and many other things. As time passed this way, I began to think that she was looking for some kind of companionship to bring increased quality and meaning to her life. I didn't plan on staying connected to her long-term, due to her "fast-lane" style of living and apparent need for frequent social contact and partying. I would much rather have spent time alone, listening to tapes, reading, meditating. At this time in my life, however, I also wanted more contact with people, and Audrey was there, and she was the vehicle. Add to that, she was fun, especially when the funny and delightful little girl inside of her emerged. That little girl seemed interested in my own inner little boy, too.

Another thing that promoted our relationship was my appreciation of the fact that she was a professional physical therapist. Our time together was good, and she shared stories of her local Catholic school experiences and upbringing. These episodes of intimate sharing were good, growth-filled experiences for me. It is curious that although we lived in the same area, were the same age, and had a lot in common, we had never crossed paths. These common roots provided us with an opportunity to share ideas, hopes, and fun.

Time passed in this way, and after about a month, I began to spend more time considering increasing my college curriculum. Audrey was a significant motivation in this connection, since she had credentials that I admired. She rekindled and fueled my already-brewing need to be more educated. By her presence, and the status I gave her in my mind, she contributed to the drive, the urgency to do better things with my life.

Therefore, in January of 1988 I began increased studies at Oakton Community College, which was near Des Plaines, where I lived, and learned word processing on the computer. I further prepared myself to join the National Speakers Association (NSA), Illinois Chapter, and become a "speaker extraordinaire." I thought, *I'll make money in speaking and put myself through college.*

The NSA is an organization of wonderful individuals who are for the most part full-time professional speakers. They run their own businesses and give presentations on every subject from motivation and sales, to accountability and leadership. I had begun my association with them by attending the NSA-Illinois bi-monthly workshops held at the Chicago Marriott Hotel. I would also speak when NSA members were showcased before hundreds of corporate meeting planners. I helped get meeting planners together to preview a sample of what the speakers could do, and what they had to offer. Each member would talk for fifteen minutes, and the planner would choose one or another speaker that satisfied his or her company's requirements.

In 1988, I began speaking professionally. People received me with open arms, and with that first talk, which was on meeting and overcoming challenges, my presentation skills took off, and advanced exponentially. Over several years, my ranking in the State of Illinois was eleventh, ninth, and fifth, respectively. That means I was always included in the top eleven speakers. For practical purposes, this meant I would be called upon repeatedly to give speeches to various groups, both in and out of state.

One summer, for example, I spoke at a Nestle Foods National Convention in Atlanta, Georgia on Lake Lanier Island. The subject was about motivation and commitment, and putting everyday obstacles into perspective. What a high! People left my talk with rekindled spirits and a renewed dedication in their personal and professional lives. And I left with that much more personal conviction that my life had meaning. Like many of my audiences, the Nestle people gave me a standing ovation. The reason for these kinds of responses, I believe, is because of the courage and hope I demonstrated, in spite of living in a severely damaged body.

Of course, behind that courage and hope was the conviction that what I had done with my life thus far, and what I was teaching, was the truth. I was coaching people on how to live a better life, by installing discipline, and by making daily efforts to address, manage, and surmount their problems. I was teaching purpose. I taught them that this could be accomplished by learning from wise teachers, by putting their sage advice into practice, and by never giving up. These were the expressions of my deepest conviction that what I had done—and what I was doing—was a stellar way to live. I had taken these pearls of wisdom from the mind and body gurus who had been willing to teach me in the first place. Now, I had become teacher.

In addition to the content of my talks, I was also developing delivery skills with each audience encounter. There is the message; then there is the presentation and the production. Audiences need humor, feeling, and inspiration. Attending a presentation is like going to the theater. People who attend a movie or a production want to be stimulated, to feel emotion, to be touched in some way. They want to have a ride, and go up and down. But, at the end of the ride, they do not want to be left down. Each presentation I did was seasoned with my growing presentation skills, and ended on a hopeful and inspiring note.

Audrey was intrigued by my proficiency as I spoke more on a professional basis. She was not a very good communicator, and appreciated what she saw me doing. I suspect this impression was what encouraged her continuing interest in me, and in her desire to spend more time with me. Although there was potential for more between us in terms of a deeper relationship and increased contact, we continued to relate more on a platonic basis, mutually inspired by each other's talents and personal characteristics.

I also liked her simple beauty. Audrey was a tall and slender young woman, who walked with a runway-model gait. She had big, beautiful eyes, with lots of white showing. Her hair was always cut in a stylish fashion, and she gave the impression that she took good care of herself.

I liked her following me wherever I went, and wanting to do whatever I was doing. It seemed she just wanted to be with me. She also knew my many needs and seemed genuinely willing to take care of me. How great is that? She also liked my discipline, my centeredness, and my will to live. I believe Audrey was nourishing her own developing inner life from the gains I had already made in my own mental and spiritual pursuits.

I will share with you a rare and precious encounter that evolved between us as the months passed. As our social contacts continued, an evening arrived in which the way we had been together changed. Normally, my helper was the one who put me to bed each night. But, sometimes Audrey would accompany me home, and we would say goodbye there, at the door. Audrey had come to my house after we had been out socializing. Rather than leaving, and letting me call my helper to put me to bed, she surprised me by offering to do the job herself. "Tell me what I need to do to help. You just tell me." She was, after all, a medical person, and I took the gesture as an act of kindness. But, I must admit that at those words, I was filled with a delicious anticipation. At a more basic level, a teenage boy inside me was thrilled! This was almost too good to be true! So, I did not object, and Audrey went about the time-consuming and rather involved process of getting me prepared for bed.

As you already know, I was now able to stand, and even walk, so after wheeling me into the bedroom, Audrey did what we called a "standing transfer." I stood up out of the wheelchair, and Audrey swung me about and down onto the bed. Next, she helped me remove my clothing, as we joked around a lot about other things, through this evening ritual. When she got me completely undressed and laid out in bed, she threw a towel over my private parts. I always slept naked because my external catheter tended to kink and leak if it was not kept free of the kind of tangles that only night-clothes seem able to conjure. Then she connected me to the overnight foley bag, and covered me up with blankets. Fully dressed, Audrey sat on the bed and we continued talking.

But, this was to be a different kind of night. Audrey eventually laid down beside me. As we continued talking, the unexpressed physical affection that we had kept at bay for so long started to brew. Before long, I was utterly non-resistant to her subtle moves. I am going to leave the rest to your imagination. All I can say is, that night was like a dream come true!

To continue the story, skip the Interview and go to the next Chapter.

INTERVIEW

Dr. T.: What is it that drives your public speaking?

M. S.: Power, prestige and profit, in that order (laughs). Though the great wisdom literature, the scriptures, the philosophers, caution us about dangerous attachments to these pursuits, I admit to being tempted by every one of them. Even though I spend a great deal of my available energy seeking to adhere to high principles and to cultivate virtues, I still feel a very human drive to attain these transient values.

Dr. T.: Are you a good speaker?

M. S.: Yes. My long years of study with the National Speakers Association, and attending seminars and workshops, have provided me with speech organization, and platform and delivery skills. I thoroughly love speaking when I feel good. The amount of preparation I must do depends upon the group, and the purpose of the presentation.

My favorite presentations involve those that are intended to change people's lives. Groups that have that kind of motivation are the best. Another good experience is being employed to provide results, such as moving an organization from adversity to cooperation, from problems to solutions.

Dr. T.: How important was your relationship with Audrey in the scheme of your other most important relationship, with paralysis?

M. S.: Our relationship was extremely significant because that connection was where I spent so much energy. I worked to grow and have a meaningful bond. I venture to say that for quads, the emphasis is on the body. With Audrey I wanted to repair my material life as much as possible. I wanted to be a normal part of society, be married, have a home and children like everyone else. Questions were always playing in my mind. Where do I fit in? How am I doing in relation to what other, so-called "regular" people are doing? Audrey was not only a significant love, but she represented an opportunity to capture these material human values.

"Life, misfortunes, isolation, abandonment, poverty, are battle-fields that have their heroes; obscure heroes, sometimes greater than the illustrious ones."

--Victor Hugo

18

TROUBLE IN PARADISE

Days, then weeks passed after Audrey spent her first night with me, and I came to discover parts of Audrey's personality and behavior that put me off. She had a puzzling need to have many people around her, paying attention to her. This concerned me. I also foresaw that I would eventually be expected to meet her family. I believed that being entangled with her would pull me ever more deeply into events and activities that could cost me precious energy.

On the other hand, I was seeking personal growth, to challenge myself to a full potential, to grow toward expressing whatever my capacity was. The idea of having a devoted woman with me and supporting me was just great. I enjoyed her attention. She was lovely, healthy, and a woman. I was a quad. Our body status dichotomy, the vast difference in our physical appearance and capacity, was disconcerting to me, however.

During 1989 and into 1990, our relationship began to show trouble, at least for me. Audrey stayed near me all the time, followed me about, and went everywhere I went. She would even show up just to watch me during my walking sessions. She wanted so much of me. Why? I talked to her, and thought about the answers she gave, and the behaviors she demonstrated. Although she expressed loving many things about me, as I did about her, I was to some extent feeling unable to measure up to an "all-out" relationship.

I came to the conclusion that she wanted to see what was responsible for my apparent inner contentment. It was clear that Audrey basked in my presence, even in my frequent retreats to stillness. What I learned was, that in spite of her being driven to seek some kind of acceptance and appreciation through her many social activities, she seemed to get her deepest nourishment in our quiet times together.

From early on she was locked onto me as a spiritual being. She had witnessed my spiritual practices that, besides regular periods of meditative silence, included spiritual reading, attending mass, and listing to inspirational speakers. She also accompanied me to weekly meditation groups that Dr. Trausch was conducting in the Chicago suburbs. She further joined me on retreats in monasteries, and on Wisconsin escapes. She was inserting herself more and more into this path I so loved. I was her living rock, even though she had other motivational resources such as audiotapes and books to inspire her. She was my girl.

Paradoxically, even though we were not living together, her close quarters behaviors became annoying for me, probably because I had necessarily learned how to nourish myself with generous helpings of solitude. It had become my daily fare, and rather than being cheerless when alone, solitude and silence had become a generator of inner energy for me. I had come to rely on those nourishing states to keep me going.

On the one hand, Audrey made me feel good about my spiritual disciplines, and this served to advance me further on this road. My self-image grew stronger and I felt increasingly better about myself because of her ability to appreciate what I valued so much.

On the other hand, Audrey was taking up too much of my time. Time was fundamental for me. I took so much time to do everything. I needed time for school, time for exercise, time for speaking, for managing my helpers, and time for just being! I also needed time to pay attention to my helper's needs. I was like a parent to most of them, looking to their emotional and physical needs, their relationships, and even their jealousy over Audrey! I had so much to do, every hour of the day. Now, Audrey's welfare and wellbeing had to be considered, and added to my already heavily laden plate. All too often this left me aggravated and feeling overburdened. What to do?

In spite of all my lamentations, I admit I still wanted to step out of what was by other measures a reclusive existence, to live a little of the jet-set life, and do some of the things that so-called "normal" people did. Audrey represented a ticket into that territory. What a quandary these two opposing forces were for me. My inner and spiritual side was at odds with my outer and material side. More weeks passed, and in spite of these dichotomies in our way of living, we spent enormous amounts of time together. It was in this environment that Audrey disclosed her interest in marrying.

I should have been thrilled with that demonstration of her affection, her devotion, and her appreciation of our life together so far. But, now I began to worry "big-time" that I would not be able to complete my bachelor's degree in psychology, having finished at Oakton Community College. What was wrong with me? Was I deluded? She was so skilled in my care, and was so affectionate, that she made it easy to grow closer together. Audrey was the one who was pushing me to marry, and a large part of me felt it would have been foolish to turn her gesture down. So, we arrived at a kind of compromise. I would continue at De Paul University and complete my bachelor's degree. After that we would marry. So, that was the plan.

During the ensuing three years at De Paul, I fairly struggled to hold her back, so fervent was she to become my wife. Although she was important to me, I realized before the marriage that she could easily get burned out with those unending daily and nightly tasks that are part of a quadriplegic's life. The loving wife would be swallowed up in an overwhelming expenditure of energy. We would have to work it out so that she could always get space and respite from taking care of me. So obsessive had I become over this concern, that after our marriage, I would keep my original home help program in place so that Audrey could fit in where she felt inclined.

While we awaited the day of marriage, I met her parents, who were both very kind to me. Audrey's mother, however, was a little suspect of me, being protective of her daughter, and perhaps not liking her dating a person in a wheelchair. I also met her nuclear and extended family at holiday gatherings. They were traditional Catholic get-togethers, and everyone seemed genuinely friendly and sincere, and cared about how I got about and how I was attended to. In July of 1995, at age thirty-five, within one month of my graduation from De Paul University, I married Audrey Jans.

* * * * * * * * * *

From all appearances, our marriage should have been sheer delight for me. But, from the beginning of our coming together as husband and wife something insidious was brewing, and it is only in retrospect that I am able to identify it. Right from the start, there was a new "spin," a new perspective that prevailed. We each had done all this work on ourselves, on our resistances, and on our hidden issues, in premarital counseling. We took workshops, had sessions with therapists, and even discussed whether or not to have children as I, hopefully, became stronger and able to accommodate a family.

But, after the wedding reception, all this high-minded cooperation ended. My impression was that Audrey needed more connection and contact, both from me, and from the lifestyle and contacts she had to some extent forsaken to be with me. I, on the other hand, needed less contact. Rather, I needed more space, more distance from couple's gatherings, more solitude from her, and in my life in general. I had no idea that marriage required such intense contact. Our marital atmosphere was like a cultural vortex in which couples had to conform to some arcane canon that said, "You must never do anything apart from each other any longer."

As the weeks unfolded early in our marriage, Audrey wanted me to pay attention to her friends as well as to her. This quite simple expectation, by itself, overwhelmed me since I had to pay so much attention to my quadriplegia. Her perhaps normal needs loomed bigger than I felt I could accommodate, and my faulty belief that I had to attend to them put that much more pressure on me. Is paying increased attention to a spouse a husband's duty upon being married? I must have believed it to be so. Audrey's increased need for attention, and my heightened need to give it to her arose from the nuptial bond and soon became pervasive.

I wondered what was happening. Did society, or genetic predisposition, or both, covertly impose these expectations into our nature? Did they lie there dormant, only to be activated upon recital of marriage vows? Most earlier, high-minded agreements, like being given large amounts of alone time to attend to my spiritual pursuits, and to study, that Audrey and I had discussed before marriage, were traded off for these attention needs after marriage.

This shift in our expectations appeared verbally at first, but soon we saw their effects in our behaviors and attitudes. For example, Audrey would ask, "Mike, can you come over to my girlfriend's house for a party on Saturday?" An innocuous, and even loving request to include me, to be with me. But, in my condition I had to be steadfastly vigilant in heading off little neglectful acts that would later come back to bite me. Falling behind in some bodily ritual like checking my catheter, or not being sure I had taken a bowel movement, was to court incalculable embarrassment, and even danger for myself. Just a simple trip to a party could be filled with trouble. Finding and getting on clothes to wear was a major project for me. Someone must undress me. Then, someone must dress me. Someone must groom me. Someone must see to my toilet needs, my liquid and food needs. My exercise needs. Even though my body so cavalierly resists moving of its own accord, it seems very much in need of being moved.

With all these concerns weighing on my nerves, I still agreed to accompany Audrey to some parties. For example, on one occasion, a man near me who had been drinking too much started to topple. In trying to catch his balance he grabbed the push handles on the back of my wheelchair, and in doing so flipped the wheelchair backwards, throwing my legs up into the air, and driving my head into the dirt. The action so startled me that I was shaking, even though I was not seriously injured.

You might think that it was no big deal. That is because you have it wired in your mind that you can take some action in your defense, no matter what the situation. But to some people it is a big deal. Think about it. We all have a startle response. Yours works for you. Mine does not. If someone pretends to sucker punch you, you react instantly by withdrawing your belly and tightening it up. For me, there is no such power. I cannot withdraw. I am at the mercy of the action.

Take another example. I am sure you have experienced sitting in a chair when someone surprises you by pulling you backwards from behind. You become startled. Instinctively, your hand shoots into the air, your legs shoot out, and you quite naturally, and quickly, lurch forward, trying to jump from the chair and regain your balance. Even if you cannot make it in time to stay on your feet, you can twist around into the backward fall and get your hands around in front of you to protect your face from meeting the dirt. For someone in my condition, there is no such response, except on the inside! As my body falls backwards, I feel the same panic run through my nervous system that you feel. Adrenalin saturates my body, as it does yours, but no outer startle response comes for me! I have no recourse except to fall backwards, my unresponsive body remaining in the same casual sitting position as I land on the ground. I suppose that I look to others like I am quite tranquil.

So, what can I do about this? Well, although my body will not respond, I have generated some inner accountability and power, and an incident like this one I have described simply reinforces my intention to avoid these situations, preempt them, and these kinds of people as well. Planning ahead for such unforeseen eventualities keeps my mind constantly scanning for potential trouble.

Without this little insight, you may think that the question Audrey asked me, her husband the quad, is a reasonable one, a natural request for a spouse to ask. But, if you have mentally crawled into my skin, and really felt what it is like not to be able to move at all, I think you will agree that circumstances like these can be overwhelming, especially if you happen to be "good natured" enough to risk placing yourself in them too frequently. Therefore, safety and survival questions keep me regular company: how will I get through the next hour? What trouble will sprout when I give myself a moment's respite from concerns? What if Audrey drinks too much, and she or her friends are unable to watch out for my welfare? I did so much want to go to parties, play with Audrey and her friends, and let myself go. I wanted to be more a part of life's flow again. But at what cost?

Another, perhaps healthier, side of me coexisted along with the party boy. Although I wanted to participate more with Audrey's active life, the other "me" didn't feel bad about not being included in these kinds of merrymaking because, having experienced them in the past, I knew the inevitable course that such gatherings took. Partygoers would initially begin with superficial chatter. After awhile, the conversation would became more noisy and scattered, focusing on gossip and celebrities, and pontificating unfounded opinions about everything. Then, when most people wearied of these mind-numbing and ineffective ways of finding some authentic soul satisfaction, they would boost their intake of alcohol and drugs. Then came the next party, and more shallow conversation, more gossip and clamor, and the inevitable mood changing chemicals.

Did people not see that their self-worth could not be improved in this way? I guess most people do not want to look at that truth. It is too much work to become awake. They would leave gatherings unsatisfied by not sharing and listening to thoughts closer to their hearts. They did not understand that it is by talking about uplifting ideas and engaging in virtuous behaviors that one's sense of wellbeing increases.

Over time I came to realize that life in general is much this way, only not as concentrated and intense as a night's party. We all seem to seek, in varying degrees, self-respect and satisfaction that is based upon appearance, prowess, power, beauty, and fresh gossip. Good feelings based upon such material values do not last for very long, but seep like sand through the cracks in ego's fragile network. It is only by learning to understand oneself from the inside out that genuine self-appreciation and wellbeing can germinate, and take root.

Many months passed, and a growing malaise had infected our life together. A time came when I would resist participating in these party activities altogether. Audrey did not seem to mind either, but later I would catch her pouting. Eventually, she too gave up wanting me to accompany her, and eventually did not even ask any longer. By then I was disappointed and saddened that it had to be this way. I needed companionship, as did she, but not in the same way. I needed someone to really be there for me, to take care of me, and just lift a bit of the load off my shoulders.

Our mounting differences and resulting distance left me without the important little things I needed help with. Being turned in bed is one example. If I did not turn in bed every three or four hours, the pressure would build up on my hip, or my elbow, or my neck. Because of so many major surgeries, I could not leave my neck in one place very long because it would stiffen and cause increasing pain.

An ironic consequence resulting from these losses in our original intimacy, and Audrey's help in my care, was that I needed to take large amounts of pain medication, which I kept close to a water bottle beside my bed at night. Because of the overall work I had done to walk independently, I had acquired partial use of other parts of my body. Arm movement for example. I used this and other such basic skills to help myself in painful and untoward situations, and to head off even worse predicaments.

To continue the story, skip the Interview and go to the next Chapter.

INTERVIEW

Dr. T.: You spoke at length about the attention needs people display. What is responsible for your uncommon insight into deep and hidden human motives that seems unavailable to most people?

M. S.: Insight grows through reading spiritual and inspirational literature, checking in with one's mentor, therapist or life coach, studying oneself and acknowledging both positive and negative qualities. This is how I live, close to high values, and when I violate those principles I experience a disturbance in my heart. Living close to my cultivated inner standards becomes both my inner joy, and an early warning system. This is the core source of my insights.

Dr. T.: Would you have failed to perceive the violation of higher values in yourself and others had you been fully functioning?

M. S.: Yes, more than likely. I would have been caught in my own insecurities, in my own deluded mind games, blindly competing for attention with others. A great eastern philosopher said: *We live in the state of our own understanding.* Going through the quadriplegic experience has brought a heightened sense of awareness to me. Although I still falter, I am aware of being in sync or out of sync with my ideals.

Dr. T.: Was Audrey just wrong for you, given your nature and goals, or is there a principle or condition that would have made your relationship work?

M. S.: If I were physically able-bodied, Audrey would have been the right person. I cared very much for both Jill and Maria, but I loved Audrey in a way that I had never experienced before. Although we had our differences, she did many of the things I liked to do, had many of the qualities I loved, such as going out for a run with the dog, sharing a theatre experience, or exploring the world together. She had a great family. What got in the way of our relationship was my disability, my slowness, having to be loaded in and out of cars, not liking the increased social activity, the coming and going that was part and parcel of my association with Audrey.

"Without stirring abroad, one can know the whole world; without looking out of the window one can see the way of heaven. The further one goes, the less one knows. Therefore, the sage knows without having to stir, identifies without having to see, accomplishes without having to act."

—Lao Tzu

19

DISRUPTIONS

Years earlier, even before my graduation from DePaul University, I had learned, along with the rest of the family, that Mom had seen a physician to have her lymph nodes tested for cancer. I wondered where in the world cancer would come from, although she had had a number of moles removed. Since she was going to see someone anyway, I wanted her to go to a specialist, an oncologist, and not the general surgeon she was consulting with. It turned out that the testing disclosed minimal cancer, and so Mom let the general surgeon whom she was seeing remove the three offending lymph nodes, along with twenty-four other, normal nodes.

Within several months, I got a shock. Mom told the family that she had to have a mastectomy because cancer had somehow invaded her breast. She was not happy about this, nor the radiation treatments she accepted as part of a cancer management protocol. But she agreed to try some alternative remedies that I had recommended, like chelation therapy, massage, and herbs — and the cancer went into remission. Months later it resurfaced, and Mom began both radiation and chemotherapy, which weakened her and left her with increasingly diminished motivation.

By January, 1996, she began to lose her grip on her identity to some extent, and regularly complained softly about not feeling well. Mostly, I recall that she stopped coming into the kitchen as much. The kitchen was our hangout place. But Mom stayed in the living room, covered with her blanket, watching TV. I saw much less of her those days, when visiting, because I could not easily roll my wheelchair over the living room carpet, so we experienced somewhat of a disconnect. I had a terrible feeling in my stomach that she had, in some way, been misdiagnosed and mistreated by the doctors, and that the original general surgeon should not have taken out all those healthy lymph nodes along with the cancerous ones, leaving her immune system compromised. My paranoia about this hearkens back to my mistrust of doctors in general because of my own experiences. Also, perhaps my siblings and I were not paying close enough attention to Mom's wellbeing, because of being caught up on our own dramas. It was not enough that my marriage was in such distress. Now, I had Mom, my everything, my support, my special person, in full-blown cancer.

Within just weeks, Mom could not remain at home, so weakened had she become. In the hospital, her doctors found that the cancer had spread dramatically, especially into her lungs. I visited her in her hospital bed, played soothing meditation music for her, and talked to her about great ideas.

A day came when her condition was worse, and she was in very much pain. I spent time telling her she could "go to glory" now, and reminded her of the many times she sat in church praying, and preparing for this event. I meditated with her and prayed for her soul, consoling her with gentle words. I still recall so vividly how, as the malignancy advanced and her suffering increased, she would sometimes just look at me in her pain and ask how I could endure my own burdens.

Neither doctors nor anyone else would tell her the truth, straight out, that her condition was terminal, so I, along with my brother Jim, told her that she was near death. My Mom never left her bed, and the next day quietly passed from her body.

In my mind, I thought that this was the best thing for her, since she would have been transferred to a nursing home, or to a family member's living room, suffering all the while. This was because the hospital would not keep a terminal patient there very long. Having spent so much time suffering myself, I did not want this for Mom.

In my heart, however, I was very sad. I tried to be strong, but cried a lot. The sadness has never left me, although it has faded over the years. It has served a purpose, however, in that it has motivated me to look more deeply into the afterlife where Mom has preceded me. I still harbor anger, wanting to blame someone, like that surgeon or someone in the medical field. I expected they would explore every way to cure her, and felt helpless because I could not do it myself. I had so much been in her position, discovering that medical science was unable to help me, and now I had watched my loved one go through it. Even though over the years I have wrestled with and reduced my own self-pity, with Mom's passing I had a new pity in my heart.

*   *   *   *   *   *   *   *   *   *

Those were difficult times. Since my marriage to Audrey in 1995, our relationship had soured, and my Mom had died. Also, during this period, I had graduated with my bachelor's degree from De Paul University in Chicago, and immediately enrolled in George

Williams Graduate School of Social Work in the fall of 1995. Could anything more be added to my plate?

In February of 1997, after about two years of emotionally debilitating conditions between Audrey and me, I broke down. During an exhausting graduate school program, which included four-hundred and fifty hours of internship, a swarm of speaking engagements, and managing a small business of special care attendants, I acquired a dreadfully invasive staph infection in my upper leg that superimposed another disability over my already-existing physical paralysis. It consumed me over the next seven months, and I had to drop out of school, cancel speaking engagements, and stop my internship. The inexorable infection made me a super prisoner in my own home, just as the original accident had made me a hostage in my own body. I could not move, and endured daily spiking temperatures of 103 to 105 degrees.

If that were not enough, the staph and its delirious effects got so bad that I needed several surgeries to stave off the infection's relentless onslaught on my life. A mass of microbes was building a nest in my leg, along with plans to take over my entire body. In one operation after another, surgeons cut me open to remove as much of the infection as possible without eliminating what was left of me, along with the microbes. Following each operation I was left with aftereffects of constant chills, a 105-degree fever, and an unrelenting companion of pain that frequently left me exhausted. Audrey now got to clearly see me as the crippled man I was. For yet another time in my life, since the hockey accident, I was at death's door.

Not unexpectedly, being in this morbid and fatiguing state for so long, I had come to the end of my energy reserves, and very much wanted to open death's door. As fate would have it, however, I was again delivered from this more prolonged near-death experience, and slowly mounted a recovery. My almost-dead body was somehow crawling its way back. Steadily, in small tentative stirrings, I began moving again.

By September 1997 I was able to return to graduate school, along with the help of my nephew, Bryan, who drove me back and forth to George Williams College in Aurora, Illinois. Since I did not like being shuttled like an invalid on this three-hour round trip journey, I made every effort to regain the strength necessary to drive myself. At night I had Bryan, take me out into an empty parking lot to practice driving, using a vehicle with hand controls. Turns. Stops. I had not driven in seven months. The boy was patient with me as I tried to gain some control over this machine. Most quadriplegics cannot drive. But, because of my ongoing obsessive work with mind/body professionals, I had recovered enough hand and arm control to manipulate a vehicle's controls. Automobile manufacturers had already made cars with hand controls replacing foot pedals in order to accommodate those who were partially handicapped. So, I was in business.

*   *   *   *   *   *   *   *   *   *

During graduate school, and through the staph attack, Audrey and I stuck it out, mostly going our separate ways as more months turned into years. Looking back, I am only now aware of the symbolic relationship between that staph infection and my ailing marriage to Audrey. No one was to blame. Our crippled marriage was a calculated risk from the start, although we did not know it. Armed with counseling and much information about how to nurture relationships, I believed that large helpings of space were necessary components in the formula for a successful and healthy marriage. Being too much together is as wearing as being too much apart. We had tried to emulate the wisdom of the brilliant philosopher poet, Kahlil Gibran, on marriage in his book, *The Prophet*:

"Love one another, but make not a bond of love;
let it rather be a moving sea between the shores
of your souls. You were born together, and together

you shall be, forevermore; but let there be spaces
in your togetherness, and let the winds of heaven
dance between you."

Regrettably, in our youthful anticipation, we did not have the seasoning, the discipline, nor the wisdom to make that formula work.

By March of 2001 we finalized a divorce that had taken a long year to unfold, and which had weakened and angered both of us. My family, too, who had loved Audrey, was not pleased. I was disheartened through it all, having witnessed a side of Audrey that was unfamiliar, and that confused me. This was not the girl that I had married, I thought. I defined her behavior during the period of our divorce as attempting to avoid looking foolish for marrying a quadriplegic and ending up splitting from him. I, on the other side, was the foolish one, unable to do what marriage required, and to meet Audrey's needs as a husband. I had failed at matrimony.

What is it in us that needs so badly to be loved, accepted, respected? To be appreciated? I wanted desperately to hold tightly to those values and vows upon which our coming together had been based. What else did I have to hold onto, especially since I had relegated walking independently to the lower levels of my priorities list? Maybe it was the ideal of a strong relationship that provided me with a sense of power and completion, rather than the actual connection itself.

*   *   *   *   *   *   *   *   *   *

As the throes of our breakup subsided, I decided to return to my Dad's home, appreciating anew how important it was to have a family. For yet another time in my life I was retreating. My penetration into the world of intimacy had left me beaten. The extended disturbances of our marriage, and the necessary attention to my partner, had drastically diminished my goal to walk independently.

So, after ending my life together with Audrey, I began to focus on my great, original values again. It took two years for me to get back my early vigor and taste for regaining and escalating movement. Yet I worried. With half a hip having been eaten away by the voracious staph virus, the idea of walking independently was itself infected with uncertainty.

Upon initially arriving back home, I discovered that my Dad did not want to have me there. Mom had passed on, and Dad had become accustomed to living alone. He had also initiated a new relationship with a woman. Additionally, he didn't want to take on the renewed responsibility for my physical care, let alone for my overall wellbeing. I felt sad about this fact, but understood it well.

We therefore looked into other places for me to live, and found a condo under construction in Des Plaines, in which the builder would be willing to build a handicap-access model for me. It would take eight months before it could be completed.

With that solution available, my Dad temporarily opened his house to me. During that stay, Dad learned that he could carry on his activities and not concern himself too much about me. In addition, I guess I began to grow on him. A transformation took place in him and between us, as his original fears eroded. More than that, he became increasingly attached to me, and by the time of my move to the newly built condo, he begged me to stay. In fact, one day he broke down and cried.

This had an effect on me. I was seeing my Dad's sensitive side, which I had never seen before. I realized that this older, feeble man who was alone and in need of attention, was just like his son! Even though we had contact from time-to-time, this vulnerable side of my dad had never made an appearance in my twenty-some years of paralysis. It felt good to see this part of him. And besides, I could always get another condo. I could not get another father. We decided together that we would live out the remaining time we had together in a somewhat closer way than ever before.

The map is not the territory, and life does not always play out according to the plan. Dad did not live up to his soulful expressions to me, and could, at times, be difficult to live with. We would fight over what time I would be home from work, or where I had been during an evening. It was a curiosity for me, that the parent in my Dad rose up and began to express itself, even though I was forty-one years old at the time, and had been doing counseling and public speaking. Quite in spite of these ongoing dramas, I came to see through them and love him for who he was at his core. Maybe the devastating experiences of marriage had seasoned me.

Meanwhile, I was still seeing able-bodied clients in my private therapy practice that I had begun after my graduation from George Williams in 2001. I was also employed with the First Step Foundation, a local organization that provides counseling and effective living skills to quadriplegics, paraplegics, and other disabled people. The Foundation's goal was to improve the quality of life for quadriplegics, family members, and friends of handicapped people. It is comprised of some of my lifelong supporters, and led by former state championship hockey teammates and others.

Family and friends of disabled people, in fact, receive more of the benefits provided by First Step than do the handicapped themselves. This is because quadriplegics in general do not really believe that their life is unalterably changed, and are seldom open to coaching or counseling, especially from another quadriplegic. Reality for them is deplorable and they must find out for themselves, through the process of living, the scope of their limitations. This disparity in specific experience is largely due to the fact that every injury of a handicapped person is different from the next. At its best, this will bring varying degrees of adjustment, but virtually never total acceptance.

In my private practice, I treat mostly able-bodied walking people. These clients are generated during my inspirational speeches to various organizations and associations. I almost never talk to handicapped groups because I don't play the handicapped game well.

What is that game? Handicapped people tend so frequently to fall prey to the "Rehab Recipe." This translates, for example, to wheelchair sports instead of focused personal development. In addition, some seek distracting situations in which they do not have to face the reality of their circumstances. They tend to not follow through with the actual behaviors necessary to make big important changes in their lives that will lead to freedom of mind and inner tranquility. They also tend not to take the advice of their mentors. Most do not even seek mentors. They are basically unwilling to make that supreme effort necessary to gain healing ground.

I know this attitude firsthand, and well! And I have fought it mightily. Although this has been my personal experience with many handicapped people, I do not intend to disparage or discount the many handicapped people who do work hard, and are heroes in their own situations.

What kind of constitution does it take to mount a lifelong fight against the plight of being consigned to a body that is inert? And, especially when all around are bodies that can walk, run, jump, and perform all manner of magic through the agency of their obedient organs and limbs?

Conversely, it is my experience that able-bodied people who come to me do seem to want to grow, especially after they have heard one of my inspirational speeches. That is generally when they approach me requesting to see me privately for life coaching, consulting, and personal development. Other ways people find me is through word-of-mouth: family, friends, and other referrals. I also have a website listed in the back of this book that showcases many of these services.

Now, it seems, I have come full circle. Traveling the gauntlet of my life, seemingly always kicking and fighting, has made me a tired, but wiser, man. Without the throes of the trip as a quadriplegic, I would have been as ignorant about people as any child would be.

I was now back home where a whole eon ago I had begun my journey. Although my arrangement with Dad was ultimately working, there were times when I wanted my own space. Having tested my ability to function away from home for so long, in and out of my marriage, I had developed a sense of independence. I had experienced life in so many of its forms.

To continue the story, skip the Interview and go to the next Chapter.

INTERVIEW

Dr. T.: Beyond the alternative interventions, what other kind of advice did you give your Mom when she was dealing with cancer?

M. S.: I gave her pointers on how to manage people, Dad, doctors, helpers, and get them to assist her in spite of their objections. These are the kind of skills I had necessarily learned in the course of my existence. I would show her how to motivate people, family members and others, to get some help. My mother was getting a taste of the difficulties that I had so long endured, and from which I learned so much.

Dr. T.: What do you do about not having your mother? Do you have a replacement?

M. S.: No. I pray to my Mom a lot, and I think of what she would have done, or how she would have handled herself in certain situations. In this way I draw on her wisdom, and translate it into my current predicaments.

Dr. T.: What was more important to you: Having Audrey as a spiritual companion, a wife, or as a physical helper?

M. S.: All of them. First I saw her as a spiritual companion, and would not likely have gotten so deeply involved with her had she not demonstrated her interest and apparent capacity in spiritual growth. In spite of the sad eventual outcome of our marriage, through the process Audrey seemed to genuinely appreciate my spiritual attitude and pursuits, and that I helped her return to her own spiritual base. I helped her get back into the Catholic Church, for example, since she had been divorced before meeting me. She had lost her sense of religion and faith. In return, she provided me with the many things I wanted: love, companionship, a beautiful woman, societal acceptance, physical security, being normal, so to speak.

Dr. T.: You said, essentially: "I very much wanted to die" while undergoing your staph infection. How bad was it, really? Did you do anything toward dying?

M. S.: It was bad. I had prepared to die. Such an occasion has happened again last night (2/18/04). I was ready to die. I was lodging in Florida for a few days, receiving hyperbaric oxygen treatments to strengthen my immune, circulatory, and other internal systems. My bladder was bleeding, internally. My helper and I did not know what was causing it. The urine flowing through my catheter was the color of cherry juice. Then it changed to the color of grape juice. Staff members at the hyperbaric center, upon my making them aware of it, sent me to a urologist. He could not see me, so I attempted to contact another urologist. After much hoopla there as well, I was eventually received at his office. There I waited two and one-half hours with no attention, even though he had been notified about my urgent circumstances. This condition had, unbeknown to me, been furtively, and insidiously, mounting over three days, with my urine very gradually turning darker red.

Having waited so long by now, I had become numbed emotionally, and was likely in the initial stages of shock due to blood loss. Still waiting in the urologist's office, I finally told my helper to NOT take me to the emergency room, but back home. My inner tolerance meter had topped out. My mood shifted toward my mortal frailty. I had had enough fighting and struggling just to stay alive. I was so weary of obliging never-ending physical urgencies, and grasping for some solution, that I quietly decided it was time to die.

I knew that if I went to the emergency room at the hospital, a whole medical militia would begin diagnostic procedures. Emergency Room doctors, not knowing about how quadriplegics work, would put me through endless testing and probing. Finally, they would offer diagnoses and treatments that long experience has taught me would not work.

So, back in my room I lay there on the bed, turning my mind toward death. My poor helper did not know what was happening, let alone what he could do about it. Yet, he busied himself with attempting to unstop my catheter, which had clogged with blood, forcing it to back up into my bladder. I took four extra strength Tylenol, shut my eyes and waited to die. I fully accepted the course this day was taking. I was ready. If I was going to expire now, this was a good way. I drifted into deep meditation and waited for the end to come. Weakened by loss of blood, and giving in to my weariness, I eventually fell into an unconscious state.

But death was not to be, for after a long period of perhaps four hours, I became conscious. The bloody urine was again flowing in the catheter, but had shifted from red to pink. During the course of the remainder of the evening the urine gradually turned back to its normal yellow color again. Somehow, my kidney and bladder function steadily recovered.

How miraculous. How devastating. How ironic! I had stopped everything—praying, worrying, and thinking. I had decided to lie in the bed and depart this life while my helper watched. Today, before my appointment with you, the nurses at the hyperbaric clinic were aghast, and had no ready medical explanation for the course my poor body had followed over the last three days. This drama had all taken place without the involvement of doctors, traditional medicine, or intervention of any kind. Perhaps meditation, and the inner physician, both of which I had acquired a longstanding relationship with, had worked their own magic.

Dr. T.: Due to these horrible and apparently uncontrollable incidents, have you made any plans to exercise even more control over your own life and death?

M. S.: Jesus said, "My kingdom is not of this earth; I decide when to lay my own life down." I am a member of the End of Life Choices Association, and have all my end-of-life papers in order and ready to go. I am a proponent of being in control of when you leave this earth. I have some backup systems ready if I get in a predicament beyond my physical control or energy capacity.

The number one reason for having end-of-life choices in place is for when I am no longer able to manage taking care of myself. This may apply to any individual in my situation who wants to be proactive in dealing with his or her circumstances, as organs fail, as one's worth as a human being shrinks, and one's sense of wellbeing diminishes. The intensely strong motivation to survive is overpowered by the encroaching weakness, and surrender is inevitable. I have often neared the place where I no longer see the value of continuing onward. This is not who I want to be. But it is the truth. So, the End of Life Choices Association literature has been helpful and consoling to me. It engenders a sense of peace within me just knowing that there are other people that think about these issues, and along the same lines as I do.

Dr. T.: Do you recommend this association to people who are suffering greatly?

M. S.: Answering that question would put me in an untenable position. I am not recommending anything to anyone. People who are in my condition necessarily learn more about how to manage their circumstances through the process of living with their condition. Decisions about how much control a handicapped person may need will be driven by his or her individual circumstances, and his or her personal motivation to take charge of end of life issues.

Dr. T.: You did not disclose to us too much about your first intimate encounter with Audrey. Although that is between the two of you, may I ask about what many may be wondering—how a quadriplegic can have a sexual encounter?

M. S.: Many male quadriplegics can get a psychogenic erection, but will not ejaculate. It so happens that I was eventually able to ejaculate. A psychogenic erection is one that is generated by the mind rather than tactile sensation or other sensory input.

Most quads can get an erection if there is a residual neural pathway between the brain and the genitals. The most important sexual organ is the brain, and what one is thinking with it.

I have a cavity in my spinal cord as a result of its being shattered by the original blow, but some residual pathways remain. With your help I retrained the residual fiber optics around the injury, and eventually those neural pathways responded to the mind/body interventions we did. For these reasons, I am able to have a sexual experience.

Dr. T.: What does a quadriplegic have to do to manage the pluses and minuses, the give and take of marriage?

M. S.: A quad must realize his strengths and weaknesses. Possibly even study them. Socrates said: "The unexamined life is not worth living." This is especially so for a quadriplegic. You can't cover up your weaknesses, that is the worst thing you can do. But, you must work on them, explain them, even use levity and humor about them rather than try to gloss over them.

Preparing for the funeral of Keith Magnuson, I was trying on a suit in a department store. I had driven alone, and was in my wheelchair. While the sales lady helped me, I had a spasm in my right leg. The sales person freaked out. I told her: "Don't worry about it. It is an interrupted brain signal. It will go away in a few minutes. That's just my Texas two-step." We both broke into laughter!

Although incidents like this mostly turn out well, with levity, people are generally ignorant of what quads go through, or for that matter, of what most people with unusual medical conditions go through.

We shall not cease from exploration, and the end of all our exploring will be to arrive where we started and know the place for the first time."

—Thomas Stearns Eliot, aka T. S. Eliot

20

FAMILY MATTERS

I reside now with an eighty-eight year old father who has a degenerating back, sacrum, and hips. Like me, he lives in pain. Like me, his movement is restricted. Losing more and more function in his arms, shoulders, legs, and back, he gets frustrated and angered by it. I am intensely aware of our similarities. At times we help each other. When he had surgery on his back recently, I taught him some of the things I know. We are like two very old men, even though I am forty-four years his junior.

When his granddaughter, Jennifer, got married, he did not want to go to the wedding. He was thinking that he looked old and broken down, and would not be able to easily move about, as the wedding activities might demand. I encouraged him to go anyway, and told him to do only what he could do, rather than feel obligated to live up to what he thought people might expect of him. He seemed to get into that idea and went to the wedding. I went too, and we had a good time together.

Although he has much to learn about human relationships, he has been good for me. He understands that we are both living a life of limitations, and that we are in this experience together. He has become more and more a friend to me, and although he is close to ninety years old, he supports me in my exercise, talks to my helpers, and provides a place for me to live. It does get a bit tense occasionally when he begins to see me as his little boy, or tries to take care of me in ways that are obsessive. Sometimes he still blames himself for what happened to me. I know all too well that the reasoning in his mind goes: *I got him interested in hockey, encouraged him, and cheered him on.*

But, in my reality, these things have no meaning. It is just the proximity of the two events — the fact that the accident occurred while I was playing hockey — that creates his illusion that one is responsible for the other. I have to believe that the providential scheme is much more sophisticated than that.

So it is only my living in the same house with my Dad, being a constant reminder in such close proximity to him, that prompts him to reflect that his beloved sport, hockey, has ruined my life. This gives rise to diverse emotions in both of us, but in these latter years, we deal with it better.

I have talked about Mom already. But, can I ever say enough? Although she is not physically present with me, she is on my mind. She was at the core of my psyche, my world, and when she died, an essential nutrient drained from me, and my world froze over. In that cold, lonely place, my strength gave way and I crashed emotionally. Considerations of my own survival flooded me as well, and I could not believe my sisters, or anyone else, would be able to accomplish the endless necessary functions that she had always handled for me.

Although my mother left this planet long ago, I still miss her so very much. Before she passed on, she struggled with the cancer, and the guessing game that cancer can be, when one is not sure just where it is, or what mischief it is up to.

I got a surprise. Almost immediately after Mom's passing, to the delight of my desolate soul, I discovered these five new "moms" moving in to shore me up. My sisters! Carol, Peggy, Mary, Janet, Joan. They had watched over me from a distance, from the outside, rather than close by, as my Mom had done. Each one of them, with her great maternal instinct, poured out blessed feminine attention upon me. Although they were not Mom, they did their best to display their love and compassion, and I deeply appreciated it. Their gentleness, ongoing concern, and help brought almost immediate solutions to many of my knotty problems. I do not know what I would have done without their support.

Then, there was my brother, Jim. What in the whole world can I say about him? He was complete. He knew so much about life. He provided me with sage advice about finances, relationships, travel, and the meaning of life. He provided me with peace of mind, just by always being available to me. He provided me with material support by assisting with fundraisers. His charming personality, exuberant nature, and positive attitude made him a delight to have in my world. In the past few years he has married, and necessarily become a little more distant from me. But, for over twenty years, Jim contributed to my existence in myriad ways.

By osmosis, his strong constitution and ever-positive attitude germinated within me and produced a determination that has made it through harrowing experiences that could otherwise have destroyed my will to live. My constant physical needs—a surprise bowel movement, a broken catheter, an urgent call in the night— were not too much for him. With a comforting word and an open-faced demeanor, he would make his appearance. His remarkably warm and understanding bedside manner has provided me with an extraordinary free state of mind, relative to my life in a quadriplegic's world.

Such a gift as he has been can be taken advantage of quite easily. But, I have been smart and careful, not to impose myself on him without a genuine need. I have often tried to make some return to him in my own way. For example, I recently got tickets to see the Chicago Blackhawks, and obtained an extra pass for him. Before he was married, when he was alone, I spent time with him, probing into his life, learning new interests, being there for him. I would ask him questions about his skiing trips, his outdoor adventures that he would relate to me, rather than me crying about how I could not do those things with him.

This kind of attempt at reciprocal care of my brother sometimes pushed my comfort zone, since I tended to avoid subjects that demonstrated what I could not do. I wanted so much to be with Jim on some of the excursions of his life. I would ask, "What did it feel like coming down that mountain? What did you do after the adventure? When did you get those new skis? What is going on in school? What new classes do you have this year? What sports league are you involved in with the eighth graders? What are their standings in league?"

Questions like these prompt many people to open up. If they are willing to talk to me about their life, I can enter into it and become a part of it. I know that people appreciate this expression of empathy, and find they are willing to open up more than they ordinarily would. I received as much from such encounters with Jim as he did. To a certain extent, I was experiencing life vicariously.

I can't say enough good about my family, in spite of all my rambling quadriplegic lamentations. Even though they were just an average, middle class family, there was no question about what they would do when it came to rallying to my aid. In the Chicago Rehab Center, staff members would immediately question newly handicapped patients about their families, knowing that the family is where core support comes from. Some families were willing to get their hands dirty; some were not.

Therefore, I do not feel like I am missing anything anymore. I am now able to see clearly my unjustified expectations of marriage, my excessive requirements around walking independently, and the futility of material pursuits. I have discovered that nothing really matters, not the money, not the material, not the marriage itself, but that the key is to love and to be loved. In the final analysis, my Dad and my family demonstrated it to me best. If they had not been there for me, I believe that instead of my life being a process of expansion and growth, it would have been one of contraction, deterioration, and bitterness. I am indeed blessed to have them with me.

To continue the story, skip the Interview and go to the next Chapter.

INTERVIEW

Dr. T.: What is the secret behind your ability to get people to work with you, to do what you want them to do?

M. S.: In order to get people motivated, I talk to them about what is happening in their lives and how they are coping. I seek to hear and understand them, more than talk about myself. I even ask them about the details, and this seems to be very engaging for them. Being attentive to their problems, concerns, and troubles, rather than focusing on mine, seems to be the secret of motivating and inspiring people.

What I do stimulates a sense of appreciation, a feeling that someone is concerned about them. The fruit of this method is that people like themselves better, and consequently display increased positive energy. The wonder is that since I contributed to producing that aura in the first place, they automatically, and quite naturally, pass some of it back onto me. It is a win-win state of affairs.

Dr. T.: From the beginning of your accident, you were dependent upon others, medical people, family, helpers, and friends. As time passed, you became more and more dependent upon helpers alone, as the involvement of family and medical personnel was withdrawn. Talk about your experience with these helpers.

M. S.: Helpers are at the core of my survival. They are ordinary people who help me with the most basic, routine, everyday boring necessities of life, such as getting out of bed in the morning, using the toilet, brushing my teeth, shaving, grooming, eating, getting medicine, moving about. Right from the start, use of helpers was problematic, and there was a long learning curve in dealing with the relationship of helper to handicapped. Of course, the very nature of the job itself requires a service-oriented person. So, servitude, of a sort, is part and parcel of what is happening from day-to-day. The helpers serve the handicapped person, and it takes almost astounding patience to be a helper.

One of my major issues was that of motivation. Motivating myself was a gargantuan task, and I had to, and still do, spend immense energy motivating myself just to get through a day. Having to motivate both myself, and my helpers as well, is quite draining on me.

Dr. T.: Your words of appreciation for what your family and others have done to help you are remarkable. On one hand I have a sense that this grateful disposition is really who you are? Or, is it rather who you have become?

M. S.: I think I am a by-product of my parents and the love inside of my family; and that is how I got this disposition. Watching the exchanges between my siblings and my parents shaped me. Recall, I am the youngest child, so I got to observe many interactions among my parents and siblings by the time I was sixteen years old. Ours was not always a happy family, but one that was always together. We searched together for drama and adventure, and with me being the last one, I got to see all this drama unfold. It was a remarkable opportunity.

Dr. T.: On the other hand, how much of this appreciation that you have and demonstrate is spawned by the injury you had to endure for so long? How much of it comes from that life trauma?

M. S.: I don't know. A percentage has been forced upon me, and other quads as well, to play the part of a victim, or to hold the family together, or to be a source of the family's strength. Sometimes I even believe that is why serious injuries and diseases occur in the first place, especially in an estranged or disconnected family. There needs to be some sort of glue to hold families together. Of course, it doesn't always need to be a trauma victim. A hero's role can do it, just as well. Both the victim and the hero are quite (unconsciously) adept at manipulating family members to get their needs met, soothe old emotional wounds, or passive-aggressively punish someone. For example, an agoraphobic client [a person that fears being in open places] who came to me for therapy was in complete control of his family, using them as one would a Yo-Yo, entangling them together by his dysfunction and inability to move about. He gradually exercised such stifling control over his mother, that because of the pressure, she arranged to bring her estranged husband back into the family.

Dr. T.: Is there a part of you that resents having to always be appreciating what family members, helpers, and others do for you because if you did not, they might leave, or at least withdraw, and threaten your survival?

M. S.: Without a doubt. It can get very tiresome. I know they want my appreciation, and at times I get weary and sick of feeding it to them. The good side of that is that I have enjoyed the times spent with them even as they enjoyed the time with me. If handicapped persons are not aware that helpers and others who serve them are looking for appreciation, then it is not quite as hard, at least emotionally. Handicapped persons should be aware of the fact that one of the reasons helpers help is for the appreciation and credit.

Dr. T.: What happens to the helper relationship, and your support, if you don't feed them appreciation?

M. S.: My own care, as well as my relationship with my caregivers, will begin to deteriorate. This would occur because they would not be getting their "appreciation" payoff. An even bigger payoff is in terms of what society infuses into caregiving. The more caregivers look like heroes, shining white rescuers, the more they will perform, stay in that mode, and keep returning for more nourishment. No one is exempt from this dynamic, and mothers and women caregivers, especially, play that unacknowledged "game" in this symbiotic arrangement, right along with their care receivers.

Dr. T.: What does that say about the great charities of the world?

M. S.: Probably that some people, perhaps many people, do good deeds for their own nourishment and recognition as well as, or rather than, to be of service to others in need.

Dr. T.: How do you manage to put up with the portion of these relationships that you sense are fraudulent?

M. S.: They quickly begin to emerge and show themselves. If they are so fraudulent that they begin to sicken me, I won't put up with them. When the degree of the caregiver's neediness, or the inner sense I have that something is wrong with the relationship becomes prominent, I call an end to it. The psychological education I have gotten provides me with a means of measuring it. When a helper becomes overwhelmed by his or her own deep-seated needs, designating me as the one who must satisfy those needs, it is time to terminate our connection.

Dr. T.: What should a handicapped person do at that time?

M. S.: He or she should take a step up, terminate the sick relationship, or move from it, if he or she can. If neither seems possible, there are other options, which include seeking experts and professionals, like me and you, to intervene. Otherwise, personality disorders like dependency, paranoia, obsession, even antisocial behaviors may begin to emerge and create greater problems.

"The bravest are surely those who have the clearest vision of what is before them, glory and danger alike, and yet notwithstanding, go out and meet it."

—**Pericles**

21

RETURN TO CENTER

For over two years, I have worked to prepare this book you are reading. That process involved deep reflections on those early days, when I, and everyone in my life, were making the adjustment to my shattered world. I was not a superstar then, and the pain of not knowing about the power lying INSIDE me was dreadful. The process of revisiting the crying and sour grapes, the guilt trips I attempted to place on family members and other people, not taking responsibility for what I did to myself, and the times I rejected accountability, was difficult. Recalling how I let people take care of my issues—insurance, bill payments, and day-to-day duties associated with a catastrophic accident, was painful. This was harsh. This was uncomfortable for me.

However, this recapitulation of my whole history has nevertheless brought new meaning to it. I have revisited the good things, the good work, too. Knowing so intimately that I have succeeded at living a good life gives me an inner satisfaction, an experience of a life well lived.

Greatness, it seemed then, lay outside of the world that I was thrust into by the accident. I am recalling that Mother Angelica, founder of the Eternal Word Television Network, said that it hurts inside your gut, or emotional center, when you reflect back in your life on choices you did *not* make, or *shied away from*, or *ran from*. For me, this equates to decisions that I should have made, but didn't.

I chose to write this book with *Dr. Trausch* because he is, among other things, a therapist, and able to get into people's minds and hearts. He has been in my skin at major junctions in my life, and has the ability to ask the right questions and get meaningful answers.

Did I find meaning? Do I know who I am? I still question that. As far as I can calculate, I am an entity carrying out some small role in a larger scheme of earthly life that inspires people to move to greater heights and meaning in their own lives. I am a dynamic organism in a changing world. I am evolving to greater heights, myself. I am working on unfinished emotional damage, and trying to stay consistent with principles of effective living. I am succeeding.

Concepts like effective living, and greater heights, have subjective meaning and therefore differ among individuals. Doing a good deed on a given day will be all that is necessary to equate to effective living for one person. For another, effective living can only be satisfied by a life filled with meaning, long-term personal growth, and service to others. Sometimes people who know me report to others that their life is better just because they are inspired by the motivated style of life I live, and the way I handle my circumstances.

I was recently at a hospital waiting for an elevator that was not showing up. With a Master's degree in social work and being a life coach, I am often in hospitals. While waiting, I rolled into the kitchen where food is prepared, and noticed the hospital's mission statement on a plaque hanging just outside the manager's office. As I read, a woman approached me and said: "Are you an inspector?" I said: "No." In a rather caustic and accusatory tone, she asked, "Who are you?" I told her I was an MSW, and while awaiting the elevator around the corner, had decided to read the kitchen's mission statement. The woman did not acknowledge my explanation, but accused me of being suspicious, and stated that she thought my intentions were to snoop! I restated that I was a MSW assessing a patient in the hospital, and, noting her intensity, asked her if something was wrong. She said she had never seen anything like "this" before. She meant me, a quadriplegic sitting reading a plaque in her territory. I asked if she wanted me to leave, using a kind and calm voice, and then, without having received any response from her, turned and rolled my wheelchair to the elevators.

Upon arriving at the elevators, the doors separated and two security guards exited and abruptly grabbed my wheelchair arms, as if to pick me up and take custody of me. They questioned why I had been in the kitchen. I explained, now wondering how my appreciation of the hospital's mission statement had turned into a frightful drama. The security men did not accept my story, nor did they let me go. Rather, they treated me as an intruder and spent the next fifteen minutes checking out my credentials, and my license plates on my van out in the parking lot. They never explained or apologized, but escorted me to my van. There I believe they came to realize that I was not a threat. They did not, however, take responsibility for being wrong.

What shall I do about this? Shall I use my influence and make trouble for the hospital by going to the CEO, or the head of security? No. My way is to stick to the simple path I have chosen, to treat others as I wish to be treated in spite of what they may project onto me. This harkens back to the values I have chosen to embrace. This is effective living. These are greater heights.

Therefore, I adjust as needed, in order to remain closely consistent with my ethical and moral values: bringing meaning to each event of every day, trying to understand others' problems and treat them with kindness, staying close to spiritual principles that answer difficult life questions.

However, the temptation to sell those values out, although infrequent, is very real. It is vital for me to remain true to myself. This is a "must" because I have already sampled the self-indulgent route, and it turns out that it causes more trouble than it is worth. It does not make me feel good inside, nor does it bring any genuine contribution to the table of life.

I was not alone as I cultivated and grew integrity and meaning in the field of my soul. I visited all manner of charismatic individuals, gifted faith healers and priests. They were the trailblazers who taught me what I know, helped me achieve doing what I can do.

From another perspective, the answers were all inside me. That is the realization they ultimately infused into me. The great souls I encountered on this journey were stepping-stones to the real answers, dormant in my very being. It is about having peace with myself, a peace born of freedom from the pervasive attachments to outcome that disturb it in the first place.

Like my high-minded teachers, I still continue to work. Along with the astonishing Mahatma Gandhi, I say, "My life is my work." In fact, it is because of my work, and the work of others close to me, that walking centers have sprouted up across the country for spinal cord injury research. In the last twenty years, there has been a paradigm shift regarding quadriplegics and walking. No longer is the focus on living with the condition, but with overcoming it. As a result, there are now many quads that walk. And, there is likely to be a walking program at a major university or trauma center in all major population centers.

I have often reflected upon where I am going. Ironically, today, I don't know that I any longer have a real goal. Certainly, I want to walk again. But, I think I have a purpose now, rather than a goal. I like to think that I have become the goal, and am just following my purpose: to live and bask in the aura of the great wisdom principles I have learned, just as I did in the steaming waters at Sealy Hot Springs. And, that this soul-generated purpose, because it is a living energy, will play some part in inspiring or serving others, whether they are wheelchair-bound, or able-bodied. This is the meaning of my life.

"Far better it is to dare mighty things, to win glorious triumphs, even though checkered by failure, than to take rank with those poor spirits who neither enjoy much nor suffer much, because they live in the gray twilight that knows not victory nor defeat."

—Theodore Roosevelt

22

THE DAY KEITH MAGNUSON DIED

A Tribute

A Conversation With Michael Schwass
December 15, 2003

Dr. T.: When you heard that Keith Magnuson was killed in a vehicle accident in Toronto, what was your initial reaction?

M. S.: I was bewildered. Then devastated. I didn't know how to react. Disbelief. I had no real feeling. Just deadness. Non-acceptance. Silence. I didn't even know how to begin to address something like that. He was such a powerful force in my life, and in the life of others.

Dr. T.: How was he perceived by the world?

M. S.: He had an international character. He was past president of the National Hockey League Alumni Association, so that most Canadian, American, and international players knew and respected him. He was also a two-time National Hockey League all-star defenseman.

Outside sports, he was a force with Special Olympics, with Maryville Academy for orphans, with the American Hearing Impaired Hockey Association, and other charitable organizations. Many in need felt his influence, and his presence was ubiquitous; he would often just show up at an event and help out. In his hands would be a raffle item or a gift. His scarred, stone-face of a hardened hockey player was an icon, and with his engaging smile he radiated welcome.

Attending to little things, he would never turn down any person who wanted an autograph. Even though he was still playing hockey full-time, he would attend as many service and charity events as time would permit. Later, when he worked full time as a key account executive for the Coca Cola Corporation, he still kept up this pace. Keith Magnuson was a Good Will ambassador to youth hockey, and they saw him as a gentle giant. He was so popular he could not walk down a street without being swamped with fans.

Dr. T.: What was the most important influence he had in your life?

M. S.: When Keith played for the Chicago Blackhawks, he was a defenseman, and would come rushing to the aid of the front-line players who were under attack. I can still recall his flaming red hair flying as he moved across the ice in the early years.

What he did on the rink for the Chicago Blackhawks, he did for me in my wheelchair. He came to my aid, and he stayed with me for the duration. Although he would not be considered a superstar, his grit and determination did make him a star. According to the Chicago suburban *Daily Herald* "Keith Magnuson was the Hawk. He made the most of heart on the ice, and the most of his life off it."

Many will mourn his passing, for he always had time for an autograph, a handshake, or a lesson on life. His face was as recognizable as any in Blackhawk history, including the great Bobby Hull. Keith Magnuson was an outstanding human being. In the words of Assistant Blackhawk Coach Dennis Savard, "We lost our chief."

Dr. T.: What was the greatest lesson you took from your relationship with Keith Magnuson?

M. S.: I think, how to conduct myself in public and in private, with poise and kindness, taking into consideration every other person as an individual and respecting them. Keith taught by words mostly, talking in such a way as to make each person feel special, and never using his celebrity status to his advantage. He was, to me, like a Mother Theresa in the world of sport.
Once, last year, we were having lunch and an older couple was sitting nearby. Keith got up, went over to them, and started asking them questions about where they came from. He told them they reminded him of his mother and dad in Canada. So, his behavior matched his words.

Dr. T.: What meaning does Keith being killed in this automobile accident in Toronto have for your life?

M. S.: That is a great question. The only thing that comes to mind is that when tragedy strikes you can shrink up and hide, or you can face it, head on. When WGN radio called me for an interview on the day of his death, I did not want to talk. I did not want to do it. I was in my own turmoil. I thought about it. I measured myself against what he would have done. If I had been killed, certainly Keith would have come forth and done this for me—gone beyond his comfort zone and honored me.

So, after thinking about it for just ten minutes, I made the decision to accept the interview. And, I am very happy I did because it was not only a tribute to him, but cathartic for me as well. I rose from my own bed of sadness, and maybe my strength helped others who loved and lost him as well. The fact is, I received phone calls from people telling me how strong I sounded in talking about Keith, in spite of my being so close to him.

Now I have a question for you. Why did this happen? What does this mean? What is the big picture in this? There are some three hundred former Blackhawks. Why take out the best one? The kindest, the most motivated, most giving of them all?

Dr. T.: Why do you ask this question? What does any of this have to do with you?

M. S.: Well, until now you have been asking the questions. Let's turn this around, and I'll put you on the spot. One of the most significant persons in my life was removed instantly.

In the case of your own son, Daniel, for example, there was a car crash, and instantly he was gone from this earth. Out of your life. With a sudden accident like this that wipes out such a significant person, how does one process that?

Keith could be here to do so much more good. We have such a terrible world we live in now, and a society that needs a man like this, so why him?

Dr. T.: Does it not seem ironic that of the thousands of sports figures we all know, few demonstrate the universal and benevolent character that Keith Magnuson did, and yet he was the one taken out?

M. S.: At this human level it makes no sense. It only makes sense at a spiritual level. Even then, it is difficult to process and to comprehend.

Dr. T.: This event must be looked at from a broader, more spiritual perspective. In this world, people who stand out because of their universal stature and evolved character, people like Mahatma Gandhi and Mother Theresa, carry a healing nature that is released when they pass on. If a sports figure is killed, he is generally remembered for his or her great game and how many points or goals were acquired over his or her career.

M. S.: I would tend to disagree with that. What I am hearing from people is just that they lost Keith. Lost a commodity, so to speak. He is no longer here. Since he is not visible, people will not be able to aspire to what he represented as easily.

Dr. T.: We are here to grow, transform, and pass on. That is what my own son Daniel did. And that is what we all do. Most people are both reluctant and unprepared to face the most important event of their lives: their dying. When a person who is prominent for wisdom and good deeds is killed, people then have that person at another level as a model of goodness to help them through. This is how society as a whole evolves and grows spiritually.

Another way of looking at it is, when such people die, their higher qualities are in a sense released, and we all recall them, carry them in our minds and hearts, and invoke them to help us live better lives. Notice, that although the *Daily Herald* recognized that Keith Magnuson was a Chicago Blackhawk All-Star, the focus of their glowing report on his death was of his character and deeds exhibited outside sports. What is there to remember and console you when an ordinary person or sports figure dies who has no inspiration, no charisma or special human kindness? To remember his shots on goal, or the number of passes he threw? Typically, only an athlete's physical accomplishments are remembered and discussed, and who he or she was as a person is quickly forgotten.

When a human being like Keith dies, a man who expressed high-minded values, human kindness, understanding, compassion, and deep respect, these values actually advance society in a way that is quite extraordinary. The *character* of a Keith Magnuson will be remembered, carried in the heart, and used for nourishment by many, just as you demonstrated today in answering my questions. Obviously, Keith Magnuson has inspired you today, even though he has left the planet.

M. S.: So, it is similar to what I went through when I was reluctant to accept the invitation to speak about Keith on WGN radio?

Dr. T.: That is exactly correct. You already carry Keith's essence, his bigness. You still have it. When he was killed, you were called to face your mortality, and to take your next step. You did it, drawing on his immortal essence. You carry him onward, in a way. Is that difficult for you? Of course it is. But, without such events, the natural inclination of everyone is to hang back, to resist, to withdraw and stay safe. Safety, and you already know this, is nowhere to be found, except deep within your own soul, within the realms of deep meaning.

Keith Magnuson goes into the community chest today, and from there into the community heart, where everyone can appreciate and partake of his mighty example, without any longer being able to focus or rely on the material things he brought with him. His life itself, not the trinkets he handed out, is the real gift we can now admire and enjoy. He brought himself. He brought his compassion.

That is the inspiration and the challenge for us: to imbibe and emulate according to our own capacity that essence of Keith Magnuson we have come to appreciate.

M. S.: What you said about Keith going into the community chest is just great. The image makes sense to me. I feel good about telling people that I am prepared to join my friends Keith Magnuson, and Coach Gary Weber, who have gone on ahead. Thinking about it in this way helps make it clear and logical, and easier to face death in a meaningful and peaceful way. As I reflect upon it more deeply, these are the potent ideas I would like to leave as my legacy, along with my positive attitude in meeting each of life's challenges.

AFTERWORD

A FORMULA FOR SUCCESS

**INTERVIEW WITH MICHAEL SCHWASS AND
DR. CLARENCE TRAUSCH ON THE FOUR P'S
FORMULA FOR EFFECTIVE LIVING**

Dr. Trausch: Michael, what are the "Four P's?"

Mike Schwass: They represent "Purpose," "Process," "Preemption," and "Prayer." This is my Four-Point game plan for facing whatever life throws at me, or at anyone, and for getting through life's tribulations. They are also my formula for partaking of the security and happiness that is born of meaning and purpose. If I can gain such qualities in my condition, with my life circumstances, anyone can.

Dr. T.: How did you come to settle on these principles?

M. S.: I spent many months, even years, in institutions as a patient, as an observer figuring out why this is happening to me, and questioning the meaning of life. And even later, I spent years doing therapy and research on the answers. I undertook twelve years of post-secondary schooling. All of these, my life's experiences, contributed to the discovery of a formula that works. Most of the work that you and I did together demonstrates, even proves, that these principles are valid, and effective.

Dr. T.: Let's get inside of them now. What is "Purpose," and how does it work for you?

M. S.: It represents finding and bringing meaning to life. Without meaning, life has no fuel, and no joy. Our purpose will pull us through when we are down. No one alone can continue to self-motivate over a lifetime. We must learn how to look inward and upward for something to pull us through our own lack of self-motivation.

Dr. T.: Talk about "Process." This concept is not so easy to understand. What does it mean to you, and how does it figure into your plan to be happy?

M. S.: It means for me getting connected to the universal flow. There is a subtle stream of life that many are unaware of, constantly flowing in the universe. It is not goal-oriented, but rather is itself the goal. We can choose to ignore it, or to join it. To ignore it is to court trouble, because this is how potential difficulties of life sneak up on us. This happens because attention is on the future, on outcomes, and not on what is happening here, now.
When we join that flow we are essentially living in the moment, and have more capacity to become aware of potential troubles. Choosing to be in and to attend to this flow translates into not having to spend most of one's energy rowing upstream looking for a relief, a goal that is somewhere in the future. Rather, it means sitting in our lifeboat and riding downstream to the waiting sea of life.

Dr. T.: Explain "Preemption." The word suggests anticipation.

M. S.: To preempt is to listen to your inner thoughts, your inner promptings. You can let troubles come and then deal with them. But, if you are getting signals that some difficulty is brewing, why not give it your attention and deal with it now, rather than later? This heads off the anxiety that would otherwise plague you until you have dealt with the issue. Be in the flow, the process. Then, preempt the signaling difficulties by facing them, head-on in a proactive way.

Dr. T.: How does "Prayer" figure into this formula?

M. S.: In the end, when we feel betrayed by others, friends, family, and are all alone, we need a contact. We can always go to the very one, the creator if you will, who has put us here for some particular reason. It is the same source of intelligence—call it God—that makes my heart beat, makes your blood flow, and makes everyone's fingernails grow, all without our conscious thought or effort. This is the Being I want to talk with. It helps me get centered and calm. Knowing that there exists a pure being that I can fully trust in, and is itself unchanging, makes peace for me.

THE FOUR P's FORMULA

Purpose

What moves you? What tugs at your heart? What is your passion in life? Find it. Feel it. Research, define, and embrace a meaningful ideal. Listen carefully, for it is beaconing to your soul. It is doing something that makes your life worthwhile. Early on, for me, it was becoming the best kind of athlete, a scoring champion. Then, after the accident, it was being the first quad to walk naturally. Now, it is to leave a legacy, a light that others can follow. You may find yourself beginning a new path, shifting to a new and higher purpose, at various junctures in your life's journey; and it may be one that others will embrace, as well.

Process

Fully engage yourself, and find your meaning within the flow, the course of each hour; not attaching to the goal or the outcome of your activities. Trust the universal process, and its major principle: that you are part of a bigger picture. I trust this process and use the Surrender Technique. I learned this particular method from Dr. Trausch. One way I use it is to forego my ego investment in overcoming, and yield to the forces I am up against. Typically, everything then begins to fall into place, into order, as the Universal Power would have it be.

Preemption

Get ahead of difficulties. Anticipate trouble before it germinates into a real dilemma. When a negative thought arises for example, head it off by revisiting and renewing your already-defined purpose, because purpose carries you through your troubling times. In this way, you counter the imminent danger in its infancy. For example, when I am beset by a troubling thought, I go into meditation. There, I visualize the problem, and place a cancel sign over it. I am then freed to ignore the temptation to worry. Sometimes, I actually modify the negative image in my mind into a positive one. In this way, you too can turn negative experiences into positive outcomes.

Prayer

Do not travel your path alone. Connect to an original author, an inner source, an ultimate confidant, God in whatever form you conceive him or her to be. Speak to One you have come to believe is always listening in your inner Stillpoint. Get a teacher to guide you, and learn to reach out in a way that is both meaningful and satisfying. Then you will always be able to rush to this original Source in an instant. I use this portion of the formula to get centered when troubles attack or overwhelm me. I go off alone and I pray. What can you do if you can't get centered? Ask for help from the other side, from saints, from angels, from those successful souls who have gone before.

Discussions with Michael Schwass on Various Subjects

On Playing The Game

Dr. T.: Looking back on these events of your life, is there any advice you would now give a teen hockey player that would be most valuable in preventing accidents?

M. S.: I think that sports help mold a person, teach how to win and lose in the game of life. Now, I would say, have the proper equipment from day one. Next to that, they must keep the proper perspective: stop thinking that they are someone special doing something special. That is hard to do today with coaches and parents so invested in the outcome of a game. Sports have become so much about money, recognition, and power. Parents today often compete amongst themselves, projecting their own issues and needs onto the players: their children. These kids then grow up entertaining the same faulty values, infected with their parents' investments in having the right uniforms, the "best" position, and subjective interpretation of the rules.

Often a sports community, be it Little League, football, whatever, is a community imprisoned in its own small infatuation with local outcome, and appearances. Competition seems to rule the world, and people all too often get caught up in acting out and behaving in infantile ways. Thus, the idea of teamwork, and the ideal of community with the earth and its inhabitants, gets lost.

However, there are signs that this attitude is changing in some respects.

Dr. T.: Provide some guidelines for parents and their children that are essential for playing a morally good, and physically safe, hockey game.

M. S.: Here are what I believe to be some very fundamental and indispensable components for playing hockey. These will apply to other sports as well:

1. Forget about winning at all costs. Such an attitude has too much destructive energy attached to it.
2. Get properly fitted equipment. Without such gear there is a higher likelihood of injury. Also, closely measured equipment improves performance.
3. Always practice in full gear. Partial gear invites sloppy movement and injuries in unprotected areas.
4. Attend an off-season training camp if at all possible. Being with professionals and good mentors is one of the best ways to form good attitudes and good performance.
5. Study and follow the guidelines of the Positive Coaches Association. These are rules for both parents and kids that set a standard of sportsmanship. They include: honoring the game; respect for the rules; opponents, officials, and teammates.
6. Play with your head up so that you are aware of what is going on. It is a sure thing that having one's head down will get you knocked off your feet. Also, having your head up engenders a positive attitude in itself, and connotes high self-esteem.

On Anger Management

Dr. T.: Explosive anger seems to be a lurking hazard, present at every contact sports event. Competition creates an emotional charge, an intensity in players that can quickly turn destructive. Since competition, winning and losing, and anger are so intimately related, do you have anything to say about anger management in sports?

M. S.: I recently spoke at a state conference on anger management in youth sports. My presentation was to explore attitude in the culture of sports in society. Typically everything originates from the family. The pre-existing competitive attitude in parents reinforces in the child a tendency for competition. A particular family's values, its ways of communicating, its crowding or alienation, its having experienced divorce, will affect a child, and create the attitudes and emotions that will be expressed on the sports field. These attitudes, in many cases, translate into powerful urges to compete.

This is the underlying psychological and logistical dynamic. It tends to drive sporting activity beyond what is reasonable, obliging some children to become professionals. If your kid has professional abilities, these qualities will emerge and develop naturally. They must. The force is in the child's nature. So, a parent's pushing that child is a projection of that parent's unfulfilled desires.

One of the core motivators in modern times is pressure on kids to achieve in sports because of the attraction of prestige and huge sums of money made available by large organizations like Nike, Budweiser, and so forth. Such external motivators, which also include intense hopes of athletic scholarships, fuel the already-brewing internal mental intensity. Therefore, the ultimate goal of becoming a professional is getting large sums of money, and getting immense attention. These unreasonable competitive attitudes and expectations can become the basis for much destructive anger on the playing field. I lay the blame at the feet of society, our own culture, and parental tendencies to place their own needs onto the lives of their children, who then live those needs out for them.

Dr. T.: So, what do you tell a young athlete who recognizes an excessively aggressive attitude in him or herself?

M. S.: I strongly suggest that boy or girl explore those tendencies with a professional: a mentor, a counselor, or a therapist. Talk about the urges, loss of control, and motives to people who know a great deal about the psychology of these attitudes and can help temper them, or better, help adjust them in the direction of more noble expressions.

Dr. T.: Did you end up taking your own medicine after the fact?

M. S.: Evidently. (Laughter)

Dr. T.: Early on, you were not aware of the lessons you are presenting to readers now. How could you have been? What would you have a good family that was like your own do?

M. S.: I don't know that they could do anything. If you don't know you have high cholesterol, how can you be aware of the need to eat differently. Freak accidents will happen. Families and athletes can read this book and measure themselves against what I am saying about attitude, intensity, competition, discipline, and anger. Therefore it is possible for people who know they have an attitude problem to study and discipline themselves more judiciously just because of experiences like mine.

Dr. T.: You seem to be saying kids have no control if their parents are urging them on. If you had read this book as a sixteen year old, would it have influenced you at all?

M. S.: Honestly, I would not likely have read a book like this. But times were different then. There was less awareness. I was already cut from my parents' mold. My unconscious mind was reading the nonverbal cues sent by my family. There is a chance that if my parents read it they could have made some adjustments. But I don't think that would be typical. Parents are living out fantasies and motives generated early on by their own families. This book will be more help altruistically. It will enlighten people to the overall issues. How much influence what I have said will have, relative to the weight of decades of family influence, remains to be seen. My intention is that this be an insightful self-help book. I can only pray that it does some good.

Help For The Handicapped

Dr. T.: You have chosen to include a section on helpers. Why?

M. S.: Because, even though this book was written for the mainstream public, it will likely fall into the hands of handicapped people as well. And, every handicapped person needs to know how to manage their help. Over the past twenty-five to thirty years, as a disabled individual, I have had many instructive and enlightening experiences that may serve others.

Dr. T.: What are some of the problems that arise in having to depend on helpers?

M. S.: Helpers become easily sidetracked, bored, and resistant. Many quadriplegics experience that their helpers often want to turn their work into a party, even while being on duty. To go to bars, get drunk, and to have fun. In thinking deeply about this, I came to realize that the lack of seeing any progress in their work with quadriplegics generated a kind of futility in them. Their job was not uplifting, and seeing so little progress, eventually they would start to implode. They would become disillusioned, and eventually turn against me, and so to neutralize that emotional charge, would want to party and blow off steam. A helper's job is not glamorous to begin with, so after awhile most helpers became disheartened and would lose interest in what they were doing. That would impinge on me in a very negative way. I necessarily depended upon them for my very existence. They could not really see it that way, and therefore didn't understand it. Consequently, they could not fathom the reality of their own very real value to me, and of the responsibility that our relationship necessarily required. Because of this, they could not stay interested and focused. This one condition in my life, apart from the paralysis itself, is a constant source of anxiety. I think many families and quadriplegics will recognize this issue.

Thankfully, this is where my psychology education and skills come into play. Beginning with Dale Carnegie seminars and ending with graduate school and a master's degree, psychology and mind education have given me perspective. I am able to see through to the basis of why people resist accountability, resist growing in awareness and responsibility, and I do not take their attitudes or behaviors personally. In this way I can, both reduce my own stress, and treat my helpers with respect and appreciation for what they can do. Additionally, I attempt to live up to the high standards I expect of them.

Dr. T.: So, you are saying that in spite of the fact that you are the one that needs the helper to take responsibility for your survival, you end up taking care of the helper. Isn't that ironic to you? Isn't there an absurdity about this?

M. S.: You are one hundred percent correct. This very day, for example, my helper drove me to church, and then back home again. Upon arriving at my house, he was bored and moping about. Over the years I have become alert to this condition, and understand it, so I flipped him the keys to the van—I have come to be able to "flip" these days—and told him to go to the mall. I said "I will be okay for three hours. Get yourself some alone time. When you have enough time away from me, you can come back." Helpers will need to be away from the heavy atmosphere and constant burden of the handicapped, otherwise, steady contact will wreck them; it will kill their spirit.

Dr. T.: You have become the caretaker. How do you feel about this?

M. S.: No one should have to depend upon another person for years, let alone a whole lifetime. It is not right. Human nature was not set up to endure this. Some caregivers seem to have a special inclination to help others, but basically helpers are doing it because they need the money and cannot find other work. I take them to games, talk about books, and make them feel like they are part of something bigger and not just a part of this rotting body. I try to give them the idea that there is something positive for their future. I have to keep showing them hope. I teach them how to live, how to meet people, how to behave with people, how to speak up and introduce themselves when they meet someone new. They have learned from my modeling and now begin to practice their own effective living skills.

Dr. T.: Have you developed a perspective to bring some meaning to this dilemma?

M. S.: It is paradoxical, but is the only way to lead a decent life: doing something to make the world a better place, to help people become better, to be an influence in the cosmic plan. Some years ago, a young man from Poland took a job as my helper. He was lazy, a daydreamer. He continually tried to take shortcuts with me, behavior that was costly to me, and I came down on him. I would instruct him when he drifted, then praise him when he behaved well. After a few years he couldn't take the intensity, and so he headed back to Poland. Two years later, just recently in fact, he called me from Poland and thanked me for helping him grow up. "Thank you so much for teaching me some of the ways of the world" he said. Then, just weeks ago, he returned to the States and actually came to see me, to thank me in person, "You have helped me grow up, to become independent." Now, I paid him money to teach him how to live. He learned his life skills from me, flew with me to cities around the country at my expense when I gave lectures and presentations. How ironic is that? That I would have to pay someone to assist me to do things I can't do, and then to teach them life skills besides?

Dr. T.: Do you think if you were not in this condition, such an unconventional exchange would have happened?

M. S.: Perhaps it was a divine setup. I have a helper now, also from Poland, who used to live in the High Polish Mountains. He was a ski patrolman, and his wife was killed on a mountaintop. Extremely distraught, he left Poland, headed to the West, and ended up in my living room. He has helped me for eight years, and during that time he has listened to me, learned the ways of the West, attached himself to my strength. Who would ever have guessed that of all Polish-Americans, this man would come off the top of the Alps and become the best aide that I have ever had. There must be some cosmic design that connected his ordeal and my nightmare, so that I became an instrument in helping him get his life together, even as he became an implement for my daily existence.

Dr. T.: Have you been mistreated or taken advantage of as a handicapped person?

M. S.: I have been deceived all too often. When entering a restaurant, often I am ushered to an out-of-the-way place like a corner that is less desirable, perhaps with poor lighting. While making investments I have been misled by people who thought that because I was handicapped I would also have less capacity to notice glaring deficiencies or inequities in contract agreements. Another form of mistreatment is being neglected by helpers and family members. This occurred just because I did not have the energy to meet their expectations of how I should respond to their ministrations to me. People need to know they are appreciated for what they give. Helpers especially resist meeting my minimum care needs, and somehow believe that because I cannot move, therefore I can be ignored. In most of these cases I simply do not have the energy to put up the kind of fight, the self-advocacy necessary to get my minimum needs met. This, of course, results in uncertainty and suffering. Also, many people, and especially helpers, find it easy to draw upon my therapeutic skills without ever seeing that counseling their problems is work for me, and that I should be paid for it, just as they are paid by me for helping me physically.

Of course, you can see that the mental and psychological services that I sell are much more difficult to measure than the very obvious physical skills helpers provide. And, even though I extend myself to them, most discount my advice anyway. Perhaps if I wore a hat saying "Counseling for Sale" like Charlie Brown's friend, Lucy, they would be more aware that they are taking me for granted. When I am out in public, I find people staring, and when I catch them, they quickly divert their eyes. People in general avoid facing me eye to eye, for that would mean having to deal with what I am. So, if I don't spend the energy to insist on being treated with equity, I don't get the respect a physically normal person gets. Everything is a fight for me, and I can never rest on my accomplishments.

Therefore, in order to make my life work I must have a devoted following, a cadre of people who have become devoted to my particular way of seeing life, which is essentially to make sure that each portion of my day is infused with some meaning, some higher purpose. Because devotees admire my values and the way I live them, or because they strive to embrace them as well, they get behind me, stick with me and treat me with respect. Without this higher-level commitment, I am lost. I need them. They need me. It's a good relationship. It is just what this book is about, and why it is being written. Meaning. Higher meaning.

On How To Live

Dr. T.: Is your life worth living?

M. S.: Whatever goals I achieved were never good enough for me. Neither, it seems, for those around me. Helpers, friends, family, even acquaintances. A belief I hold is that I had some hand in choosing my circumstances in order to overcome feelings of never fitting in. I wanted to be as normal as everyone else was, both before as well as after the accident. That motivation has endured. Much of my so-called good attitude has essentially been an ego defense motivated out of partial fear and partial ignorance. I needed, and still need, to maintain human relationships, to get recognition, to fill desires. So, I can see how I unconsciously threw up many of these mighty obstacles for myself, and then strove to overcome them in order to prove that I was acceptable.

Dr. T.: You spend much of the little time you have in daily life ministering to both healthy and handicapped people. Why?

M. S.: I minister mostly to healthier people, actually. And, it was no coincidence that I spent so much time with the aging and dying, especially during my graduate school field practice. Adolph Coors III summarizes my philosophy when he says: "If you live for the next world, you get this one in the deal, but if you live only for this world, you lose them both."

Suffering and dying is as much a part of this life as pleasure and living. Medical people, as well as those trained in life-saving, are accorded too much liberty to influence life and death, enlisting at times even barbaric methods to save a life, to keep someone alive at any cost. I disagree with this philosophy, even though I am a product of it.

Dr. T.: Are you more reconciled with the idea of being mortal than when you were younger?

M. S.: Yes. But near the very end we become afraid of the dying process, no matter how much work has been put into dealing with it. Death itself is not so bad for people who face their own mortality. Yet, the process of dying itself may hold much suffering, a notion that creates anxiety. It is easier, however, when you have looked deeply into the issues around dying. I have done that by studying the process of dying. I peek at it in my mind occasionally, without remaining there and overwhelming myself. On the outside, I often visit Mom's grave. I also go to funerals, and people actually seek me out as a speaker at wakes, funerals and other such events. These should not be morbid things, but gentle reminders of our own mortality.

Dr. T.: How would you like to die?

M. S.: I have asked to be taken during the night in the middle of my sleep, through a stroke, heart attack, or aneurysm. I am informed enough to know that only a certain percent of people, perhaps thirteen percent, are taken that way. I don't want to linger, however, and I have taken steps to reduce the chances of a lengthy dying process.

Dr. T.: Are you prepared to die?

M. S.: I've learned first-hand that a body can outlast its ability to function. Further, sometimes the spirit outlasts the body's ability to keep up. I have spent many nights during which I did not expect to live until the next morning. I don't fear death. I do fear a worsening condition—medical interventions, a continuing existence in a life impossible to live in. I have been ready to welcome death for a long time.

Dr. T.: Do you visit death?

M. S.: I sometimes meditate on it; go to that moment of death. Sometimes to my own funeral. It gives me a sense of freedom and peace. Also fearlessness. I recently bought a gravesite next to my Mom. I pay thirty dollars a month for it. I sometimes go there in mind, or go there in person and sit on that plot and talk to spirit, heaven, God.

Dr. T.: Do you recommend this as a way of personal, spiritual, empowerment?

M. S.: I don't recommend anything around death to anyone. If someone is enduring a terminal illness, I can give advice as to how to manage and navigate through it to some sense of peace. But each case is unique, and needs to be treated that way.

Dr. T.: Speak about the relationship between depression, and facing (or avoiding) one's mortality? You have faced your own mortality. What do you imagine would have been the result if you had never faced it?

M. S.: First of all, I believe that many times depression is a consequence of knowing too much about life's meaninglessness, and dwelling on it. In that case, depression is a generator of thoughts of death.

Not facing my mortality in a proactive way would have produced pain, agony, and certainly a lack of peace. Not knowing there is a way out, that there is a realizable end to this lifetime can, in situations like mine, be overwhelming.

Curiously, being a misfit is perhaps more distressing than paralysis and all its difficulties. This is unique to a later onset of paralysis, or for a burn patient for example. One wants to fit in again. I believe this need is different than for someone who is born paralyzed and never knew any other way.

Therefore, I am grateful for having had the opportunity to face my own death early. The alternative is to live a healthy life, and never having thought about deeper issues, have death stare you in the face. I have had the opportunity to question my existence, and to deal with and accommodate those hard questions: Who am I? Why am I here? Where am I going?

Dr. T.: If you had to do it over again, would you want the choice to be permitted to die after the accident happened?

M. S.: It is not as simple as thinking back and deciding which would have been best: to live or die. Neither is it simple to choose having or forgoing the choice. In those early years after the paralysis, and periodically throughout most of my subsequent years, an important part of me wanted to die. These feelings are true, I am sure, for many people who have their bodies taken away from them in the prime of their lives. If I had died early on I might have missed lessons in this life that are important for my overall growth, and for my lasting happiness. I don't want to second-guess what happened back then, nor the power of the universe to bring me what I needed. I wasn't given the choice. I accept that. I don't blame the accident. I don't blame the players. And I don't blame the game.

ABOUT THE AUTHORS

Michael Schwass, MSW

Michael Schwass is a member of the National Speakers Association. He has been speaking professionally for more than twenty years. He specializes in inspirational opening and closing presentations. Speech topics revolve around helping organizations meet and overcome their challenges.

Michael also maintains a private practice of consulting and life coaching for "able bodied" or "walking" people, where he works with clients on human relations, managing stress, and developing personal effective living strategies. He graduated with distinction from DePaul University and achieved a Master's Degree in Social Work from George Williams College specializing in Mental Health.

Michael was totally paralyzed from the neck down at the age of sixteen, the result of an ice hockey mishap. After many years of therapy, hard work, and determination he became the first complete chronic quadriplegic to walk naturally. He also serves as a counselor for the Chicago based First Step Foundation, which seeks to improve the quality of lives for quadriplegics, paraplegics and their families. Michael works and resides in a northwest suburb of Chicago.

Dr. Clarence P. Trausch, Ed.D.

Dr. Clarence P. Trausch, Ed.D. C.C.H., graduated from Northern Illinois University with advanced degrees in education and psychology, and is certified in Clinical Hypnosis by the American Board of Hypnotherapy. He is a graduate of the Gestalt Institute of Chicago, the Self-Realization Fellowship, and the Biofeedback Institute of San Francisco. He is a former monk of the Divine Word Missionaries religious order. His outstanding accomplishments and community service earned him "Man of the Year" award from the Veterans of Foreign Wars.

Dr. Trausch is a faculty member of the University of Phoenix, and the Institute of Transpersonal Psychology, where he teaches counseling psychology, insight meditation and East-West philosophy, and the psychology of wellness. He is a Life Coach Consultant, meditation instructor, spiritual director, and Mind/Body Medicine practitioner. He is a Keynote speaker, and workshop leader, and his most popular inspirational and motivational presentations include "How To Attain Inner Power", "The Key To Excellence", "Becoming Self-Actualized", and "Inspiration: The Breath of Happiness."

In his motivational workshops, and individual sessions as well, Dr. Trausch reveals and applies the wisdom principles fundamental to great success, and personal and spiritual happiness, acquired through his own experiences in living and studying with masters in the West and in the Far East. In individual sessions, he crafts personalized formulas for growing personal happiness, and economic success in any endeavor. Businesses, organizations, and government groups have enjoyed his penetrating insight and charismatic delivery of life's most important values: Wisdom, Power, and the pursuit of personal and spiritual excellence. He lives in and works from his home in Redding, in Northern California.

More About Dr. Clarence Phillip Trausch

Clarence Trausch began his journey at age twenty, spending eight years as a religious monk in the Divine Word Missionary order. Following this early mind/body/spirit discipline he worked for ten years as a police criminal investigator in Cook County, Illinois, while obtaining advanced degrees in psychology, leadership, and education. Additional postgraduate studies include Gestalt psychology, hypnotherapy, and biofeedback.

Upon receiving master's and doctoral degrees from Northern Illinois University, he founded and directed the Center for Counseling Arts, a psychotherapy and exceptional living center in the Midwest where he worked for ten more years.

During this time he traveled extensively in the Far East, living and studying meditation and applied philosophy with teachers of universal wisdom principles, experiences that further contributed to his professional skills, and consequent growth educational services. Upon returning to the United States he practiced psychotherapy and applied philosophy, teaching in several graduate schools, and presenting principles of empowerment to businesses, organizations, and individuals.

Dr. Trausch uses his years of academic education, professional training, and uncommon global experiences with masters of personal empowerment, to generate creative solutions to life's personal and spiritual problems. His workshop entitled "The Secrets of Personal Empowerment" present those esoteric wisdom principles along with practice of them. His inspirational and motivational keynote speeches represent the essence of his lifelong pursuit to discover the secrets of uninterrupted happiness.

CONTACT INFORMATION

Contact Information for Consultations and Presentations
Michael Schwass, MSW
P.O. Box 2973
Des Plaines, IL 60017-2973
Phone: (847) 699-6454
Fax: (847) 699-6452
Email: mschwass@mikeschwass.com
Website: www.dontblamethegame.com

Contact Information for Consultation and Presentations
Dr. Clarence Phillip Trausch, Ed.D. C.C.H.
P.O. Box 992674
Redding, CA 96099-2674
Phone: (530) 241-3880
Email: Dr.ClarenceTrausch@charter.net
Clarion33@charter.net
Website: www.drclarencetrausch.com

QUICK ORDER FORM

Website Orders: www.dontblamethegame.com

Phone orders: (847) 699-6454

Mail Orders: MSA Publications
P.O. Box 2973
Des Plaines, IL 60017-2973

Fax Orders: (847) 699-6452

Fax or mail this complete page, with money order, check, or/credit card information to the above address or fax number.

Name _____

Address _____

City _____ State _____ Zip _____

Telephone _____

Email _____

Don't Blame the Game $21.95

Plus sales tax, shipping & handling, please add $6.95

Total   **$28.90**

Number of copies _____

Payment: ☐ Check ☐ Visa ☐ MasterCard

Name on Card_____

Cardholder's Address _____

City _____ State _____ Zip _____

Cardholder's Phone # : _____

Card Number _____ Exp. Date ____/____

Please send more FREE information on:

Speaking/Seminars _____ Consulting _____ Other Books _____

Direct Contact for Presentations or Consulting:

Michael Schwass, MSW   (847) 699-6454
Clarence Phillip Trausch, Ed. D   (530) 241-3880

GIFT ORDER FORM

Website Orders: www.dontblamethegame.com

Phone orders: (847) 699-6454

Mail Orders: MSA Publications
                  P.O. Box 2973
                  Des Plaines, IL 60017-2973

Fax Orders: (847) 699-6452

Fax or mail this complete page, with money order, check, or/credit card information to the above address or fax number.

Send _____ copies of "Don't Blame The Game" to:

Name _____

Address _____

City _____ State _____ Zip _____

Telephone _____

Email _____

Don't Blame the Game $21.95

Plus sales tax, shipping & handling, please add $6.95

Total   **$28.90**

Number of copies _____

Payment: ☐ Check ☐ Visa ☐ MasterCard

Name on Card _____

Cardholder's Address _____

City _____ State _____ Zip _____

Cardholder's Phone # : _____

Card Number _____ Exp. Date ____/____

Please send more FREE information on:

Speaking/Seminars _____ Consulting _____ Other Books _____

Direct Contact for Presentations or Consulting:

Michael Schwass, MSW   (847) 699-6454
Clarence Phillip Trausch, Ed. D   (530) 241-3880